Rita Foelker

amazing Origami for Kids

Happy Fox
BOOKS

Amazing Origami for Kids © Snake SA 2018

This edition © 2022 Happy Fox Books, an imprint of
Fox Chapel Publishing Company, Inc., 903 Square Street,
Mount Joy, PA 17552.

First published in Italian in 2018 by
nuinui® a registered trademark of
Snake SA, Chemin du Tsan du Péri, 10, 3971
Chermingon, Switzerland

Editorial director: Federica Romagnoli
Editorial coordinator: Paolo Biano
Editor: Maria Pia Bellizzi
English translation: Freire Disseny + Comunicació
Graphic design: Marinella Debernardi
Graphics manager: Stefania Costanzo
Cover graphics: Marinella Debernardi
Origami sheet illustrations: Vu Kim Ngan
Illustrations: Pretty Vectors / Shutterstock.com
Web support: QL Tech s.r.l., Milan

978-1-64124-149-6

To learn more about the other great books from Fox Chapel Publishing, or to find a retailer near you, call toll-free 800-457-9112 or
visit us at www.FoxChapelPublishing.com.

We are always looking for talented authors. To submit an idea, please send a brief inquiry to acquisitions@foxchapelpublishing.com

Fox Chapel Publishing makes every effort to use environmentally friendly paper for printing.

Printed in China
First printing

Scan the QR codes with a smartphone or a tablet using
the camera or a QR scanning application to access the
videos.

To access the video tutorials for all the projects, visit:
www.nuinui.ch/video/it/L27/simpatici-origamoni

To download and print additional copies of the
patterned origami papers in this book, visit:
http://www.nuinui.ch/upload/simpatici-origamoni.pdf

CENTRO DIFFUSIONE ORIGAMI
CASELLA POSTALE 28
27011 BELGIOIOSO (PAVIA)
e-mail: info@origami-cdo.it

The publisher thanks the Origami Diffusion
Center for its valuable collaboration. For
almost 40 years it has brought together
Italian origamists and encouraged the
exchange of experiences among enthusiasts.
www.origami-cdo.it

TEXT AND DIAGRAMS BY
➡ **Rita Foelker**

PHOTOGRAPHY BY
➡ **Dario Canova**

Gemma Turnone
(origami artist)

VIDEOS BY {

Paolo Biano
(production)

contents

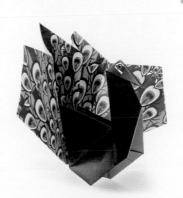

introduction

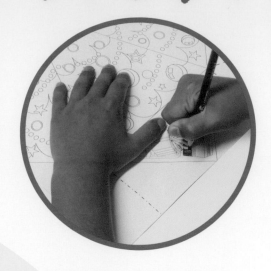

The art of folding paper is a **really fun activity!** If you haven't folded much origami before, you are sure to agree after you have made some of the projects in this book. I have spent decades researching and studying origami, and now I have proof that its creative potential is amazing. Here is what you will find in these pages! The projects are divided into four sections.

"Reading Is Fun" will help you to create original bookmarks to use in your favorite books. Creating the projects in this section merges two activities—folding paper and reading—which not only exercises the motor skills in the brain, but also exercises the imagination and exposes the reader to interesting new ideas and stories.

Create your story and bring it to the stage!

A tip for parents: If your child is very young, help them by folding and unfolding the project yourself first. This way, your child won't have to pay close attention to exact fold lines and will finish folding their origami in the blink of an eye. Work on a smooth, hard surface, and don't forget good lighting.

"An Origami Zoo" is where animals are created. Going all the way back to origami's origins in Japan, you'll learn that origami very frequently recreates subjects from the natural world, like animals of different species, trees, and flowers.

"Finger Puppets" offers characters for a story that develops as you fold the origami. You can create a different story every time, including tales involving other characters like kings and queens, princes and princesses, or whoever you can imagine!

Finally, **"Children's Dreams"** presents some toys that are much loved by children all around the world. Folded paper and imagination: these are the two ingredients for transforming daydreams into reality.

Thanks to the folding done by a talented young origamist—someone who folds origami!—there is a **video tutorial** (available by link or QR code) for every single project in this book. These videos are a wonderful tool to allow children to understand and easily follow each folding step.

types of folds

On each of the sheets provided, the folds are already marked. A dashed black line means **fold forward**, the easiest and most natural fold, where you bring the edges of the paper up toward yourself. A red line with alternating dashes and dots means **fold to the back side**, where you fold the edges of the paper down away from yourself. I tried not to use too many folds like this, since they're a little less instinctual for children.

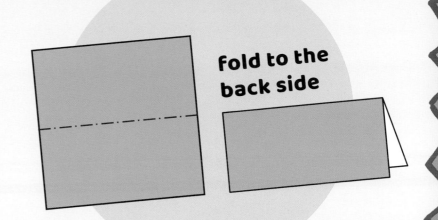

fold to the back side

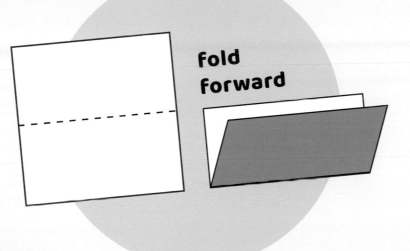

fold forward

how to orient the paper

Before beginning to fold any project, you have to correctly orient the paper. On the sheets provided for each project, **a small black dot** indicates the side to place facing up before starting to fold, as well as the edge or angle that should be at the top once the paper is placed on the work surface. (It's not always the illustrated side that starts face up—it's often the back side of the paper!)

9

reading is fun

Reading is not only fun—it is also a great way to learn through other people's stories and adventures, whether real or imagined. Unfortunately, we are less and less interested in reading these days, because it is easier to watch a movie or play a video game.

Even though there are many ways to find answers to questions and learn about new topics, reading is a necessary activity to develop critical thinking skills, good communication, and the imagination.

To help you with this, I have included here some beautiful and unique origami bookmarks that, in addition to marking the page where you stopped reading, make nice accessories for your books and will brighten up the time you spend reading.

Pick a project and get to work!

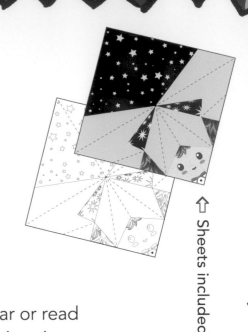

⇦ Sheets included

1 fairy bookmark

Fairy tales are truly magical! They improve the lives of those who hear or read them. Not only do they teach us valuable lessons, but they also leave an imprint on the imagination that will last forever. **Cinderella** had the friendship and protection of a fairy godmother. Three little fairies took care of **Sleeping Beauty**. Fairies are always kind and caring, using their powers to entertain and cheer people up.

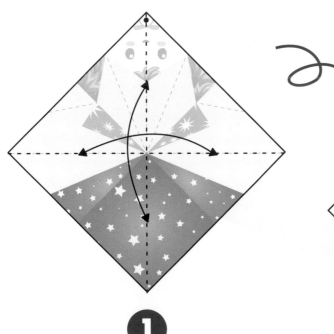

1

FOLD IN HALF ALONG THE DIAGONAL LINES, THEN UNFOLD.

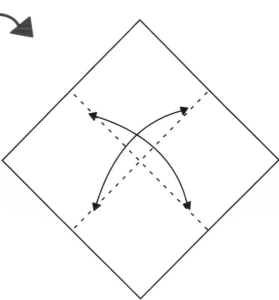

2

FLIP THE SHEET OVER, FOLD IN HALF ALONG THE CENTER LINES, THEN UNFOLD.

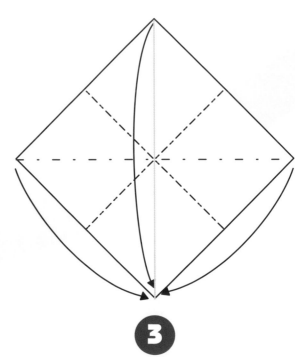

3

USING THE FOLDS ALREADY MADE, FOLD THE TOP CORNER DOWN TO THE BACK SIDE AND EACH OF THE SIDES IN TO CREATE A SQUARE.

4

FOLD THE SIDE FLAPS INTO THE CENTER.

5

FOLD UP THE LOWER MIDDLE EDGES TO CREATE THE FAIRY'S HAT.

6

YOUR FAIRY BOOKMARK IS COMPLETE!

DIFFICULTY

1

VIDEO: www.nuinui.ch/video/it/L27/simpatici-origamoni/p14

2 boat and cat bookmarks

This **boat-shaped bookmark** reminds us that reading is an adventure, a journey sailing through the world of your imagination. When you read, you can dream with your eyes open; you can **visit far-away places** and encounter the lives and stories of the people who live there. And what **better companion** to have alongside us while we sit cozily reading in a chair (or sail the seas!) than a cat?

DIFFICULTY

1

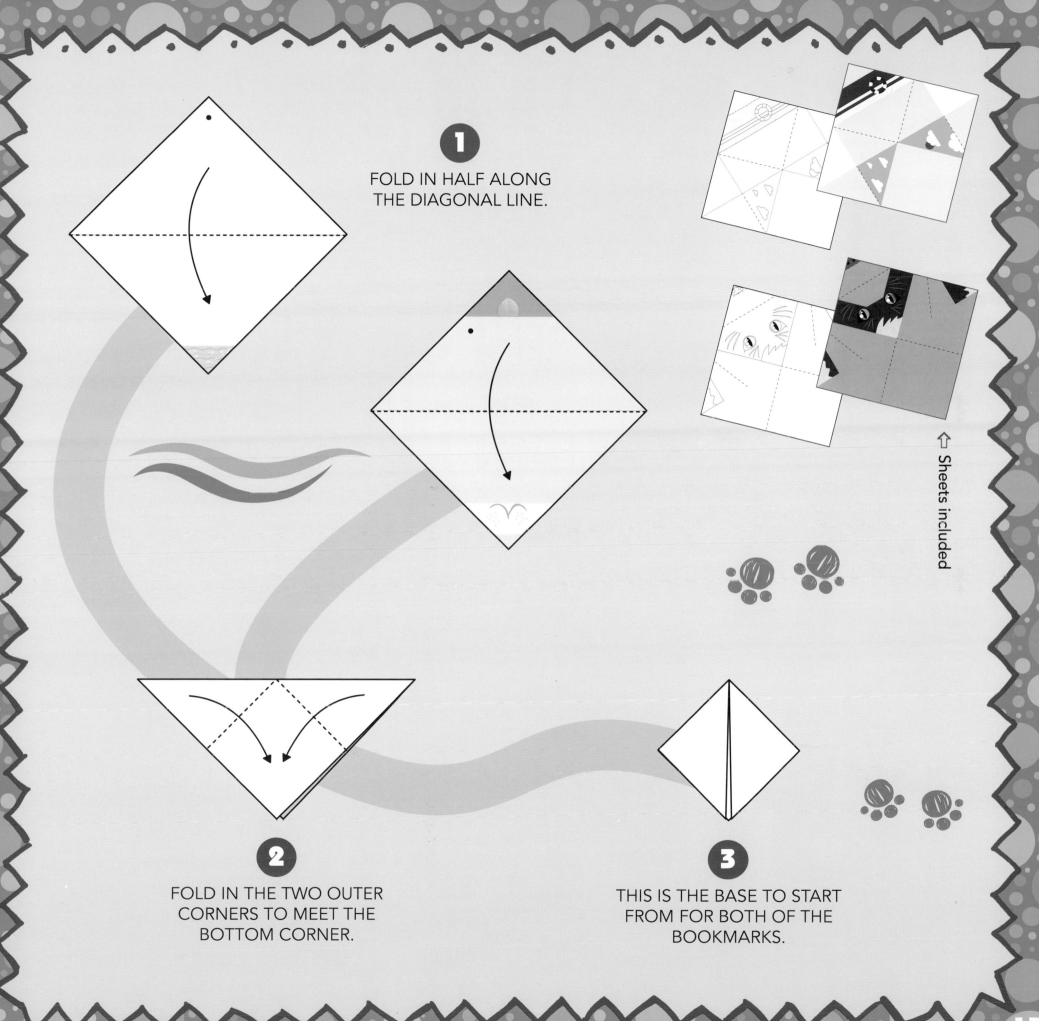

1

FOLD IN HALF ALONG
THE DIAGONAL LINE.

Sheets included

2

FOLD IN THE TWO OUTER
CORNERS TO MEET THE
BOTTOM CORNER.

3

THIS IS THE BASE TO START
FROM FOR BOTH OF THE
BOOKMARKS.

boat bookmark

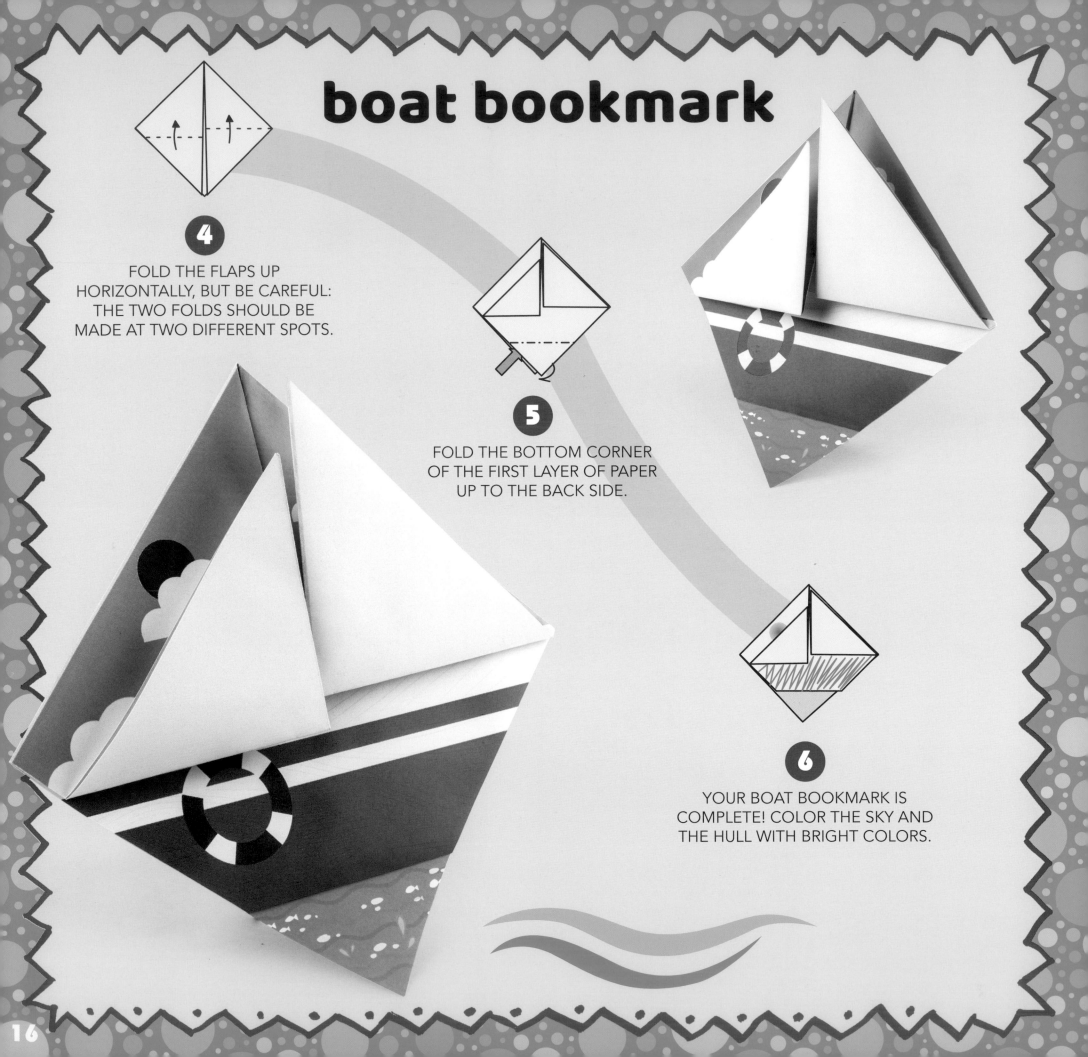

4

FOLD THE FLAPS UP HORIZONTALLY, BUT BE CAREFUL: THE TWO FOLDS SHOULD BE MADE AT TWO DIFFERENT SPOTS.

5

FOLD THE BOTTOM CORNER OF THE FIRST LAYER OF PAPER UP TO THE BACK SIDE.

6

YOUR BOAT BOOKMARK IS COMPLETE! COLOR THE SKY AND THE HULL WITH BRIGHT COLORS.

cat bookmark

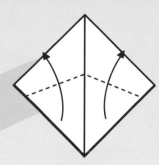

4

FOLD UP THE FLAPS FOLLOWING THE ANGLE SHOWN.

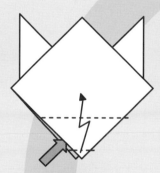

5

FLIP THE PIECE OVER. FOLD THE TOP LAYER OF THE BOTTOM CORNER UP, THEN FOLD THE VERY TIP BACK DOWN TO FORM THE NOSE.

6

YOUR CAT BOOKMARK IS COMPLETE!

3 grasshopper and heart bookmarks

One of the first tales I remember is the fable of the ant and the **grasshopper**. Fables are stories that have a moral, in which the main characters are often animals that speak and behave like people. Each of these animals has its own personality and is capable of **intense feelings**. In short, they all have a **heart**.

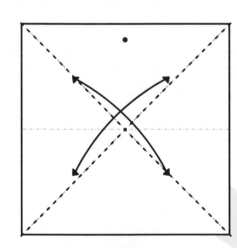

1

FOLD IN HALF ALONG THE DIAGONAL LINES, THEN UNFOLD.

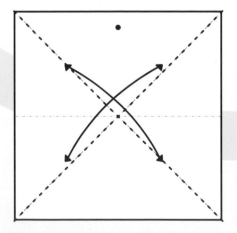

DIFFICULTY

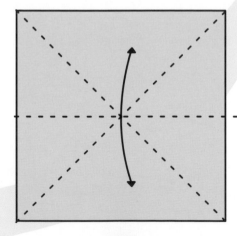

2

FLIP THE SHEET OVER, FOLD IN HALF ALONG THE CENTER LINE, THEN UNFOLD.

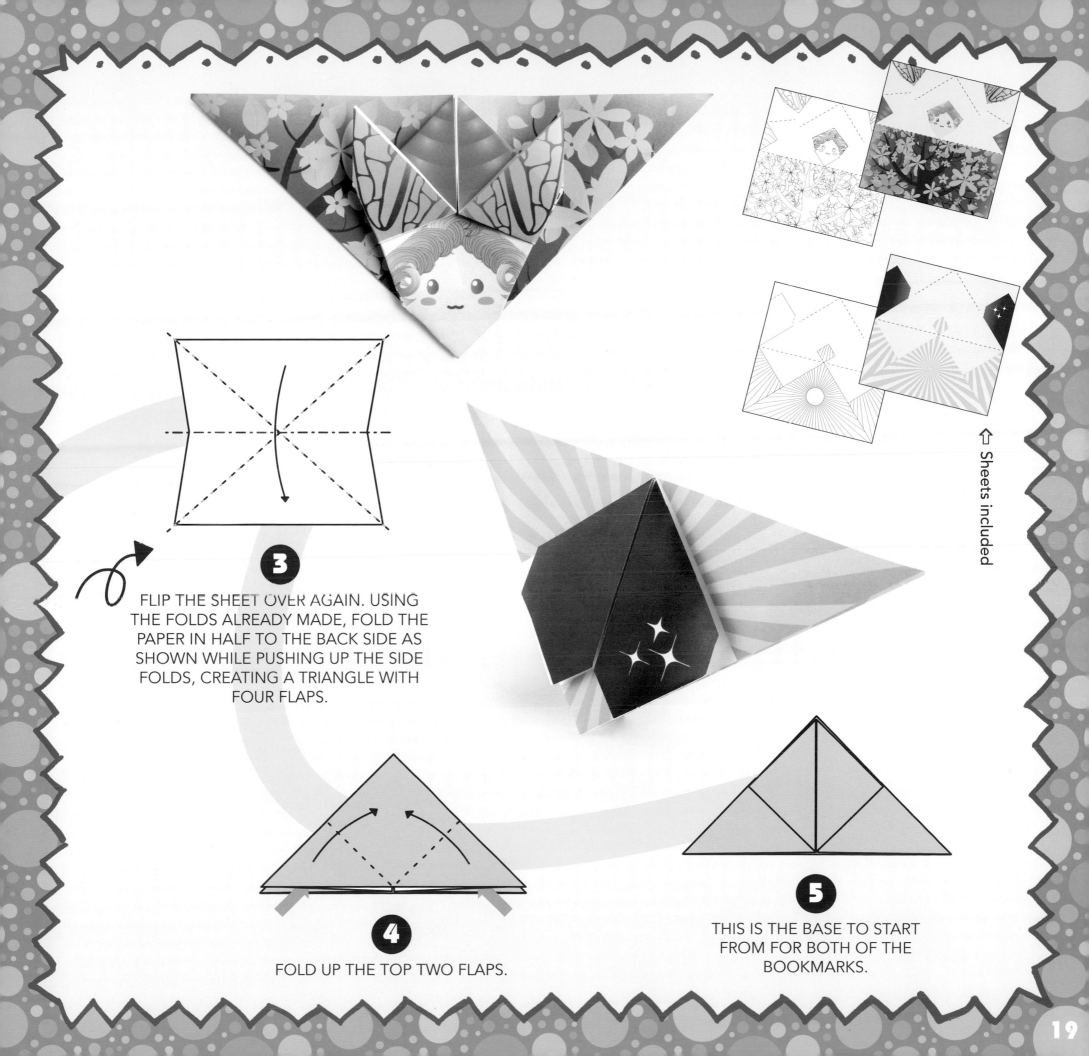

↑ Sheets included

3

FLIP THE SHEET OVER AGAIN. USING THE FOLDS ALREADY MADE, FOLD THE PAPER IN HALF TO THE BACK SIDE AS SHOWN WHILE PUSHING UP THE SIDE FOLDS, CREATING A TRIANGLE WITH FOUR FLAPS.

4

FOLD UP THE TOP TWO FLAPS.

5

THIS IS THE BASE TO START FROM FOR BOTH OF THE BOOKMARKS.

grasshopper bookmark

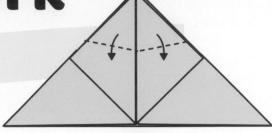

6

FOLD THE TOP POINTS DOWN AT THE ANGLE SHOWN.

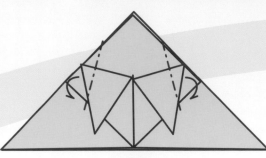

7

FOLD THE TWO SIDES OF THE GRASSHOPPER TO THE BACK SIDE.

8

YOUR GRASSHOPPER BOOKMARK IS COMPLETE!

heart bookmark

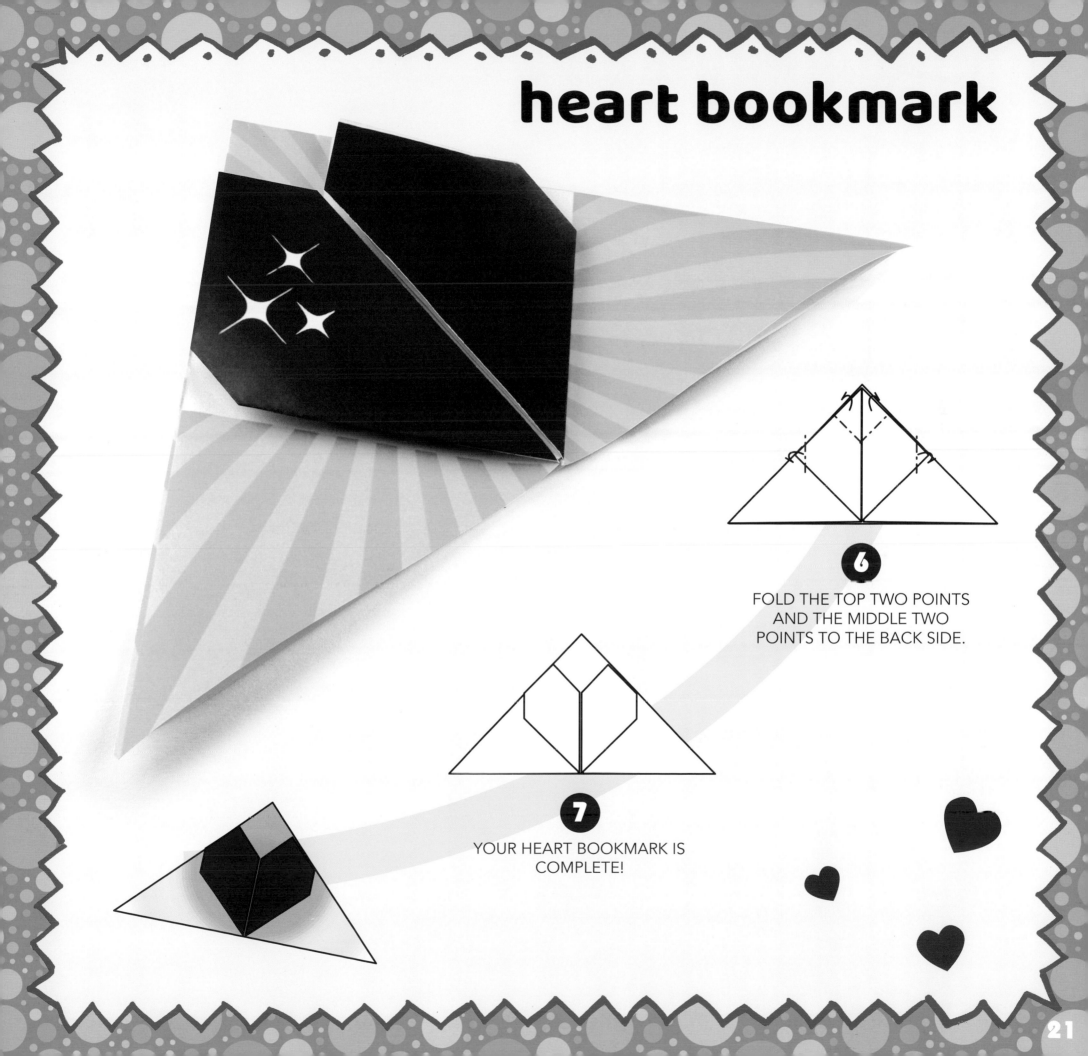

6 FOLD THE TOP TWO POINTS AND THE MIDDLE TWO POINTS TO THE BACK SIDE.

7 YOUR HEART BOOKMARK IS COMPLETE!

⇧ Sheets included

4 bird bookmark

Reading can enable you to get your wings and **fly away**. This bird bookmark is a reminder of this. Even on days when you stay home, when you read a book, it will **transport you** to incredible and **fantastic places**.

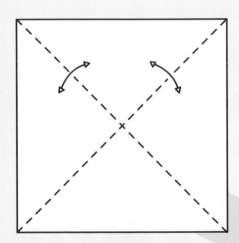

1

FOLD IN HALF ALONG THE DIAGONAL LINES, THEN UNFOLD.

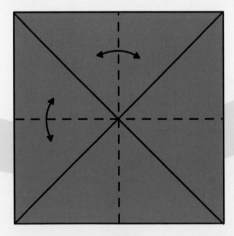

2

FLIP THE SHEET OVER, FOLD IN HALF ALONG THE CENTER LINES, THEN UNFOLD.

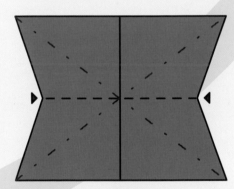

3

USING THE FOLDS ALREADY MADE, FOLD THE PAPER IN HALF AS SHOWN WHILE PUSHING IN THE SIDE FOLDS, CREATING A TRIANGLE WITH FOUR FLAPS.

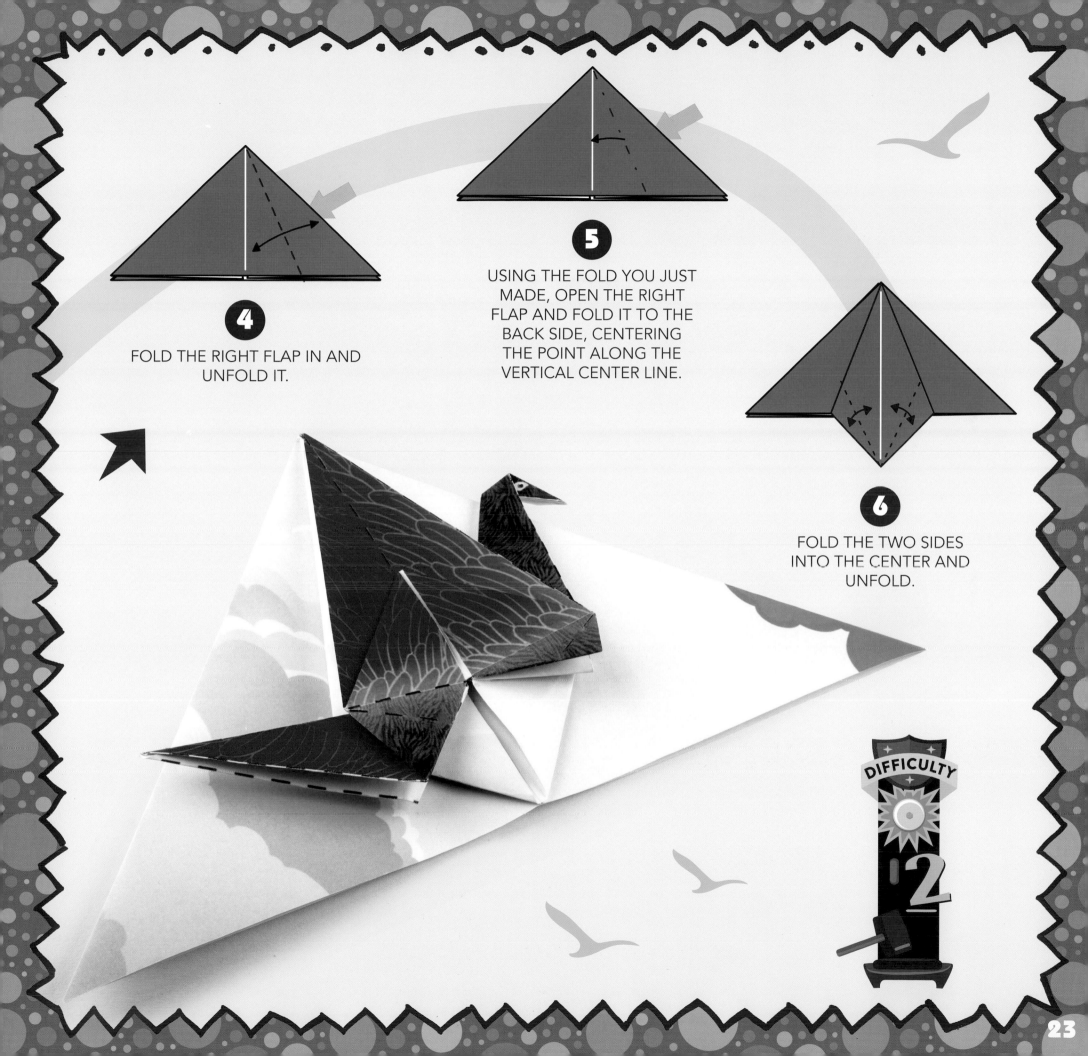

4

FOLD THE RIGHT FLAP IN AND UNFOLD IT.

5

USING THE FOLD YOU JUST MADE, OPEN THE RIGHT FLAP AND FOLD IT TO THE BACK SIDE, CENTERING THE POINT ALONG THE VERTICAL CENTER LINE.

6

FOLD THE TWO SIDES INTO THE CENTER AND UNFOLD.

DIFFICULTY

2

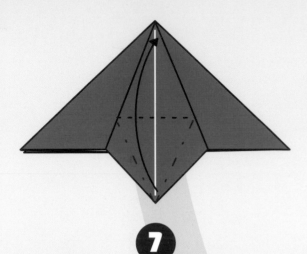

7

FOLD THE BOTTOM CORNER UP
USING THE FOLDS JUST MADE AS A
GUIDELINE.

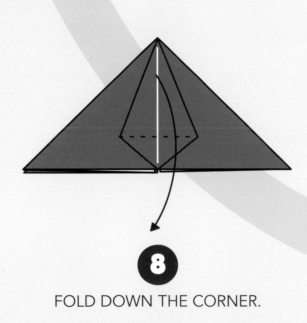

8

FOLD DOWN THE CORNER.

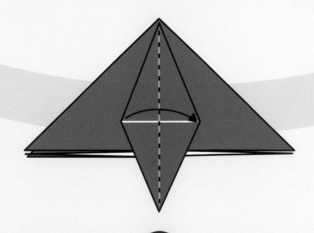

9

FOLD THE LEFT SIDE OF THE
MIDDLE SECTION TO THE RIGHT.

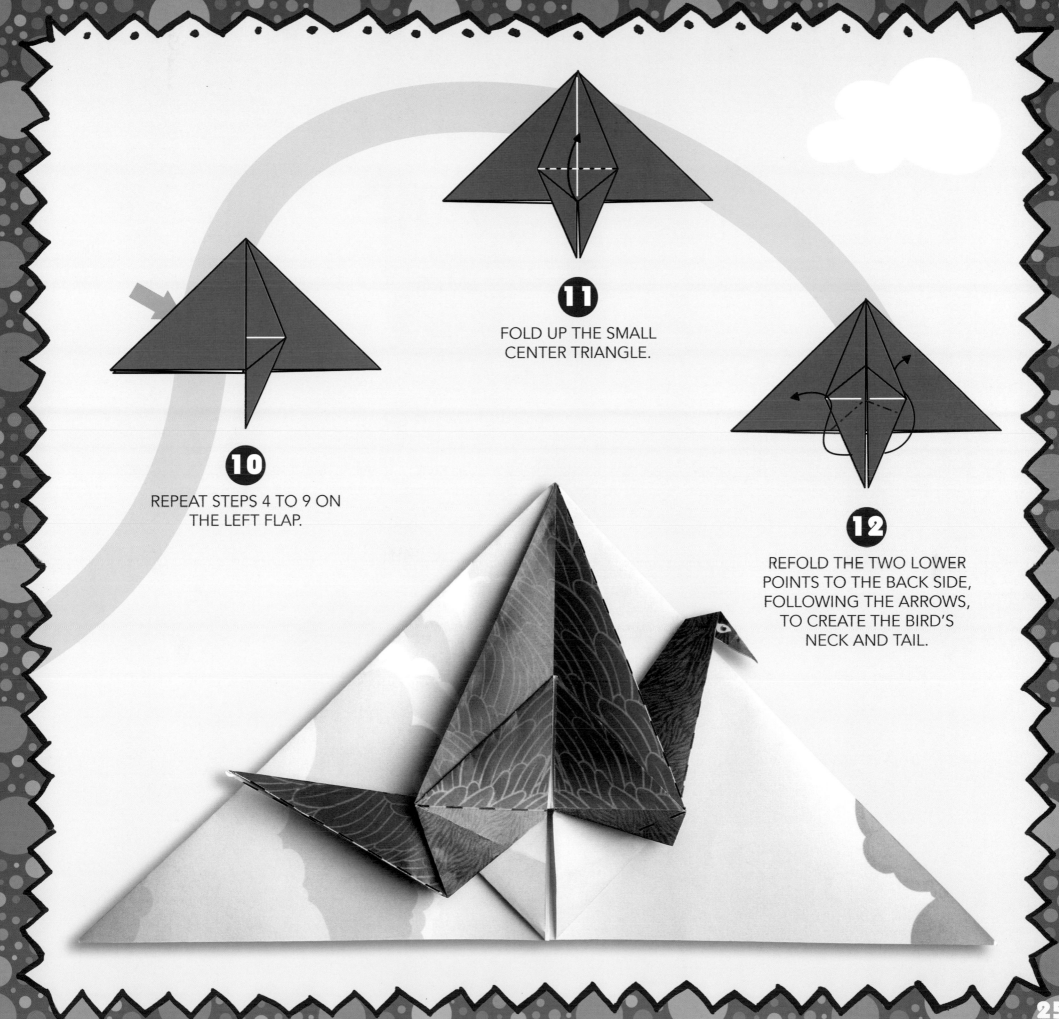

11

FOLD UP THE SMALL CENTER TRIANGLE.

10

REPEAT STEPS 4 TO 9 ON THE LEFT FLAP.

12

REFOLD THE TWO LOWER POINTS TO THE BACK SIDE, FOLLOWING THE ARROWS, TO CREATE THE BIRD'S NECK AND TAIL.

13

FOLD THE POINT THAT HAS THE BEAK TO THE BACK SIDE.

14

YOUR BIRD BOOKMARK IS COMPLETE!

12

JUST BY CHANGING THE ANGLE OF THE LEFT FOLD IN STEP 12, YOU CAN CREATE A "TSURU" BOOKMARK, INSPIRED BY THE CRANE ("TSURU" MEANS CRANE IN JAPANESE). THE CRANE IS THE INTERNATIONAL SYMBOL OF ORIGAMI.

13

FOLD THE POINT THAT HAS THE BEAK TO THE BACK SIDE.

14

YOUR CRANE BOOKMARK IS COMPLETE!

an origami zoo

One of the things that intrigued me most when I discovered the art of origami, and which has always fueled my curiosity, has been the way that origami allows us represent animals in paper. I first studied traditional Japanese models, like the classic crane, and then studied animal projects from other origami masters.

Eventually, I began to devise my own projects, which I have published in several books. If you search the Internet for "animal origami" or "dinosaur origami," you will find a whole world of origami figures out there!

In this section, I share with you some new animal projects that I have recently created and that I love very much.

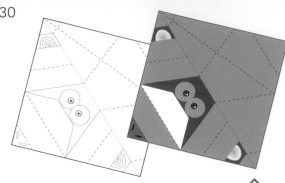

⇧ Sheets included

5 chimpanzee

I created the **chimpanzee** origami one day when I was folding a traditional origami paper cup. I continued to **fold and refold** the paper until I found a satisfactory shape for this project. I hope you like it too!

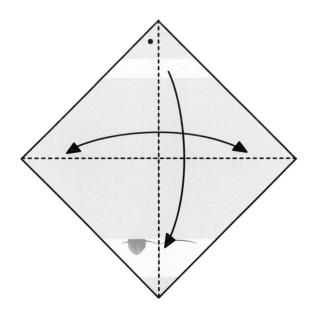

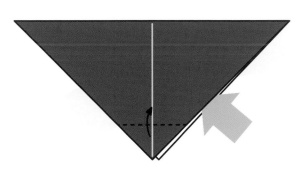

1

FOLD IN HALF ALONG THE DIAGONAL LINES, THEN UNFOLD. FOLD IN HALF ALONG THE HORIZONTAL FOLD.

DIFFICULTY

1

2

FOLD THE FIRST LAYER OF THE BOTTOM CORNER UP.

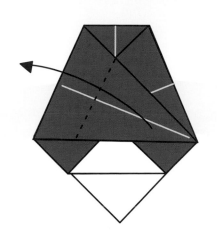

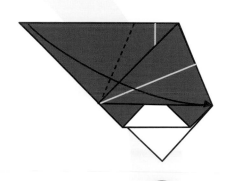

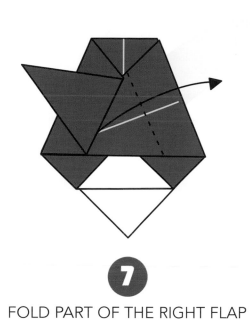

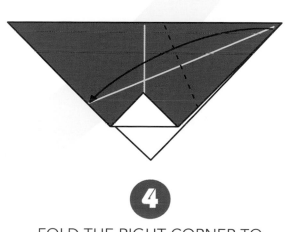

6

FOLD PART OF THE LEFT FLAP
BACK, USING THE FIRST CENTER
FOLD LINE FOR REFERENCE.

7

FOLD PART OF THE RIGHT FLAP
BACK IN THE SAME WAY.

5

FOLD THE LEFT CORNER
TO THE OPPOSITE EDGE.

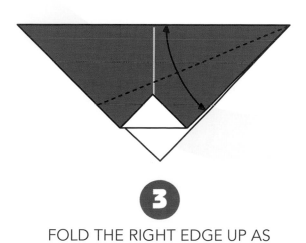

4

FOLD THE RIGHT CORNER TO
THE OPPOSITE EDGE.

3

FOLD THE RIGHT EDGE UP AS
SHOWN, THEN UNFOLD.

8

FOLD IN THE TWO CORNERS OF
THE EARS.

9

FLIP THE PIECE OVER. FOLD A
SMALL PART OF THE LOWER
CORNER TO THE BACK SIDE,
THEN FOLD THE ENTIRE
LOWER HALF UP.

10

YOUR CHIMP IS COMPLETE!

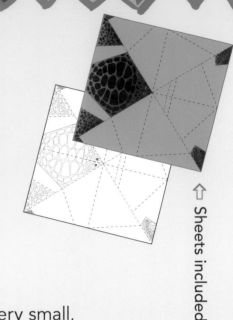

⇧ Sheets included

6 sea turtle

Sea turtles are fascinating creatures. When they are born, they are very small, but they can grow to become **very big**. Many species are endangered, and we have a duty to respect and take care of them so that they can be born, grow, and reproduce. As a reminder of the **importance of protecting nature**, I created this project, which is easy but beautiful.

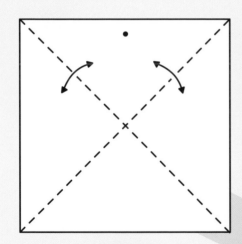

1

FOLD IN HALF ALONG THE DIAGONAL LINES, THEN UNFOLD.

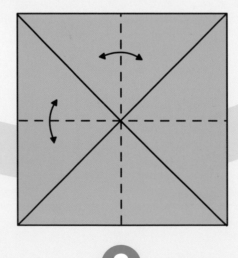

2

FLIP THE SHEET OVER, FOLD IN HALF ALONG THE CENTER LINES, THEN UNFOLD.

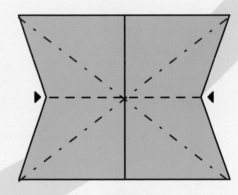

3

USING THE FOLDS ALREADY MADE, FOLD THE PAPER IN HALF AS SHOWN WHILE PUSHING IN THE SIDE FOLDS, CREATING A TRIANGLE WITH FOUR FLAPS.

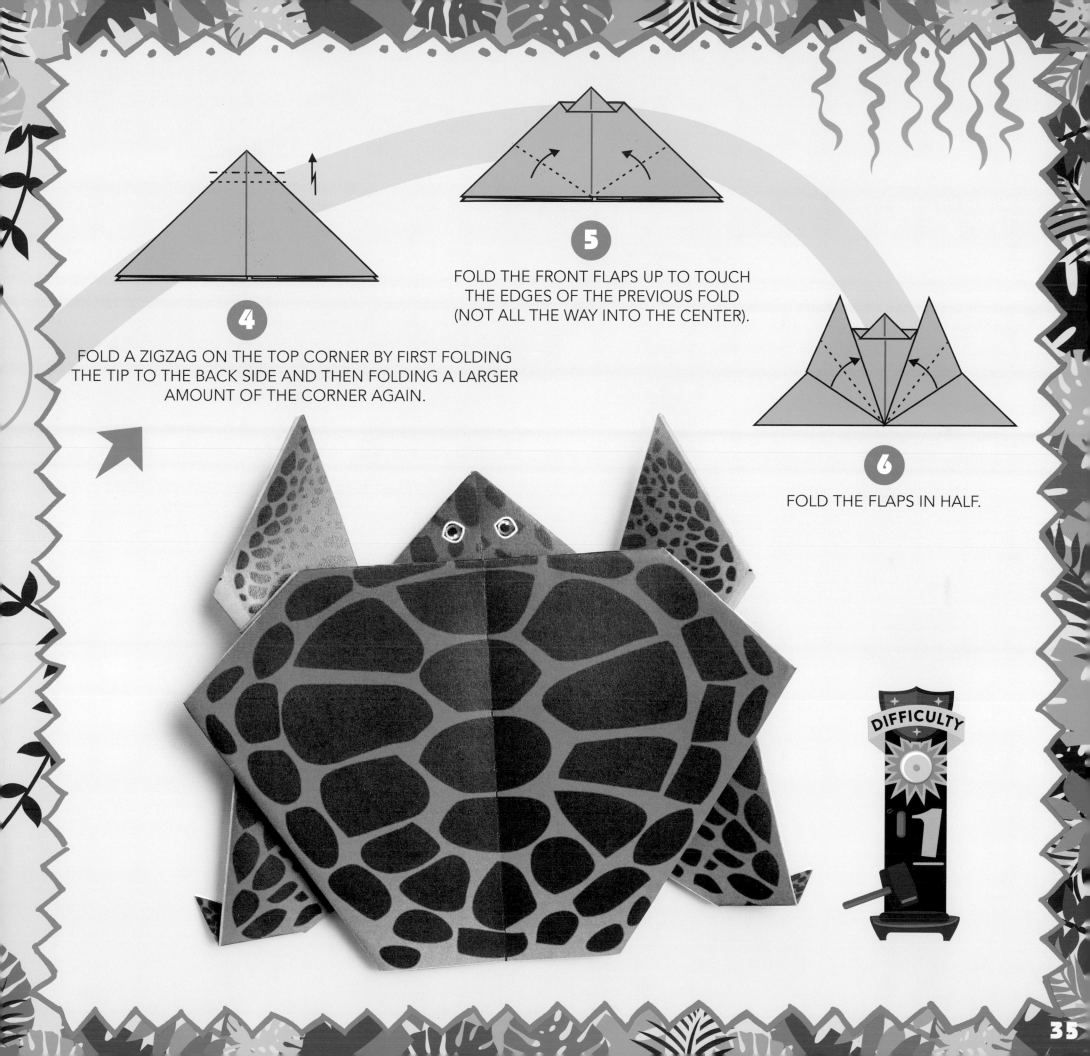

4

FOLD A ZIGZAG ON THE TOP CORNER BY FIRST FOLDING THE TIP TO THE BACK SIDE AND THEN FOLDING A LARGER AMOUNT OF THE CORNER AGAIN.

5

FOLD THE FRONT FLAPS UP TO TOUCH THE EDGES OF THE PREVIOUS FOLD (NOT ALL THE WAY INTO THE CENTER).

6

FOLD THE FLAPS IN HALF.

DIFFICULTY

1

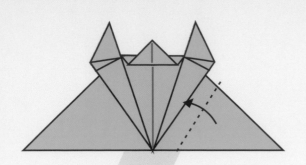

7

FOLD THE LOWER RIGHT
FLAP UP.

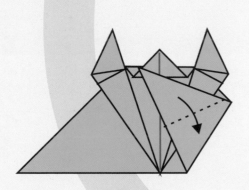

8

FOLD THE CORNER OF
THE FLAP DOWN.

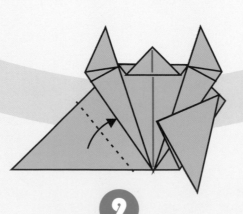

9

FOLD THE LOWER LEFT
FLAP UP.

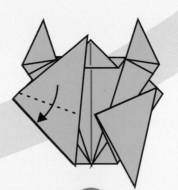

10

FOLD THE CORNER OF
THIS FLAP DOWN TOO.

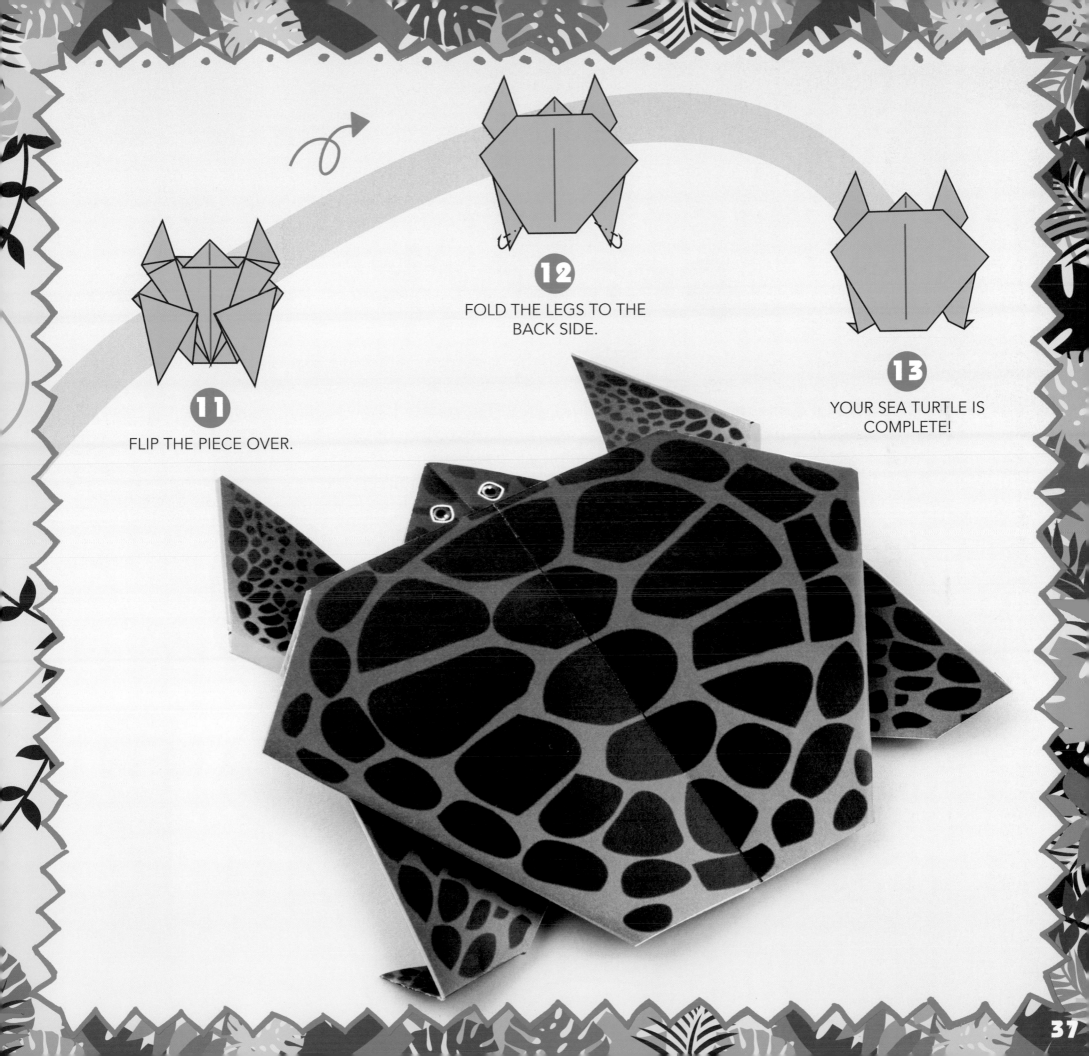

11

FLIP THE PIECE OVER.

12

FOLD THE LEGS TO THE BACK SIDE.

13

YOUR SEA TURTLE IS COMPLETE!

7 peacock

The peacock is an exotic bird and is considered a **sacred animal in India**. His large and wonderful tail attracts attention not only for its size but also for its colored feathers in **shades of blue, green, and gold**. His preferred way to rest is sitting perched in a tree. I already knew some examples of peacock origami, but I decided to create a new one that was very beautiful and yet very simple to make. He is made with two separate sheets that are put together at the end.

body

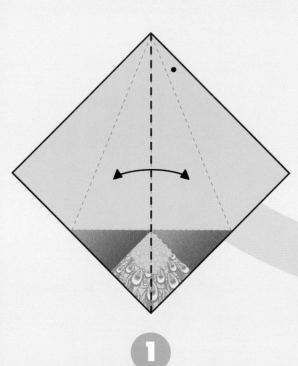

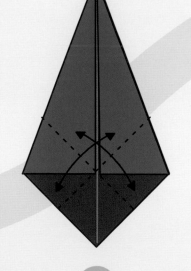

1

FOLD IN HALF ALONG
THE VERTICAL DIAGONAL
LINE, THEN UNFOLD.

2

FOLD IN THE SIDES TO MEET
THE CENTER LINE.

3

FOLD UP EACH BOTTOM EDGE
AS SHOWN, THEN UNFOLD.
FLIP THE PIECE OVER.

DIFFICULTY
2

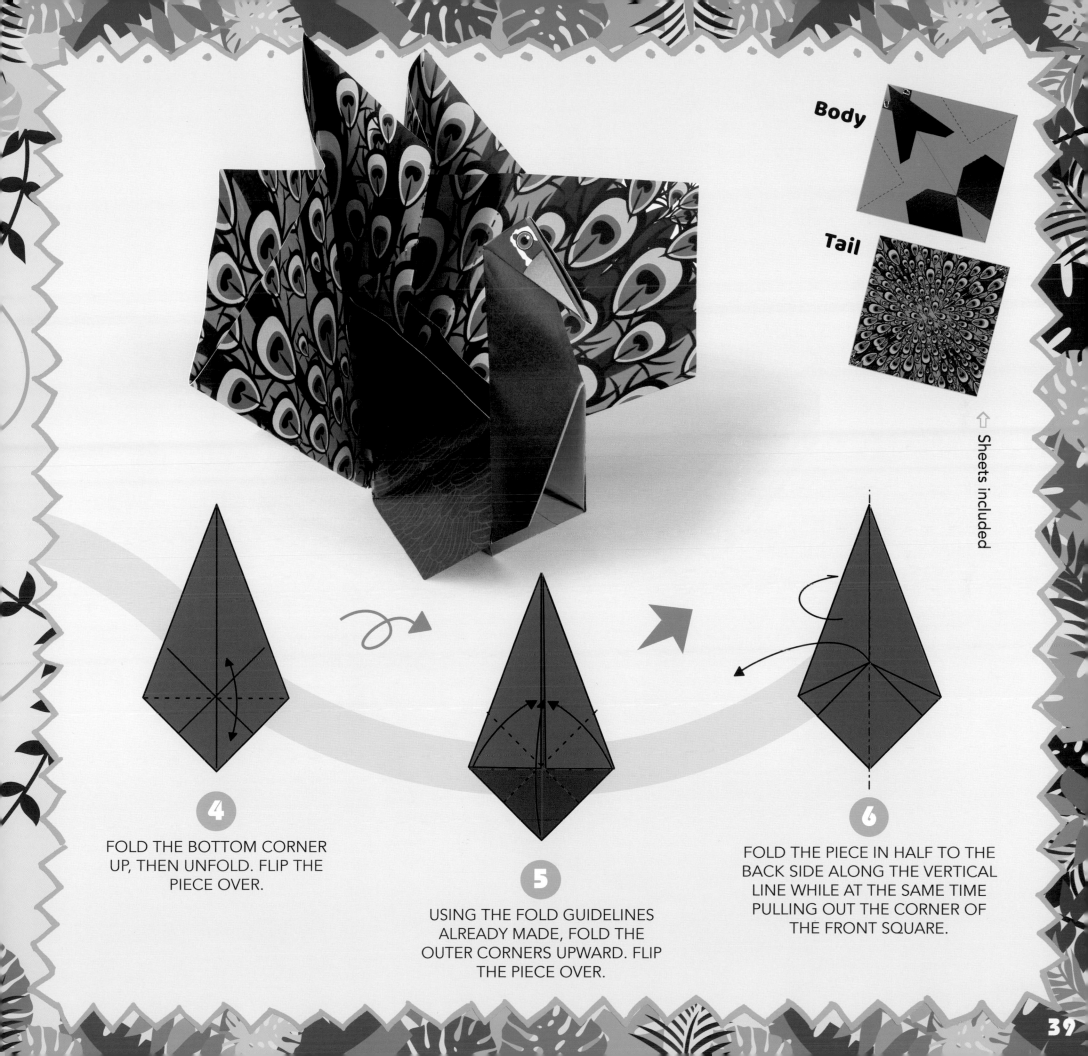

Body

Tail

⇧ Sheets included

4

FOLD THE BOTTOM CORNER UP, THEN UNFOLD. FLIP THE PIECE OVER.

5

USING THE FOLD GUIDELINES ALREADY MADE, FOLD THE OUTER CORNERS UPWARD. FLIP THE PIECE OVER.

6

FOLD THE PIECE IN HALF TO THE BACK SIDE ALONG THE VERTICAL LINE WHILE AT THE SAME TIME PULLING OUT THE CORNER OF THE FRONT SQUARE.

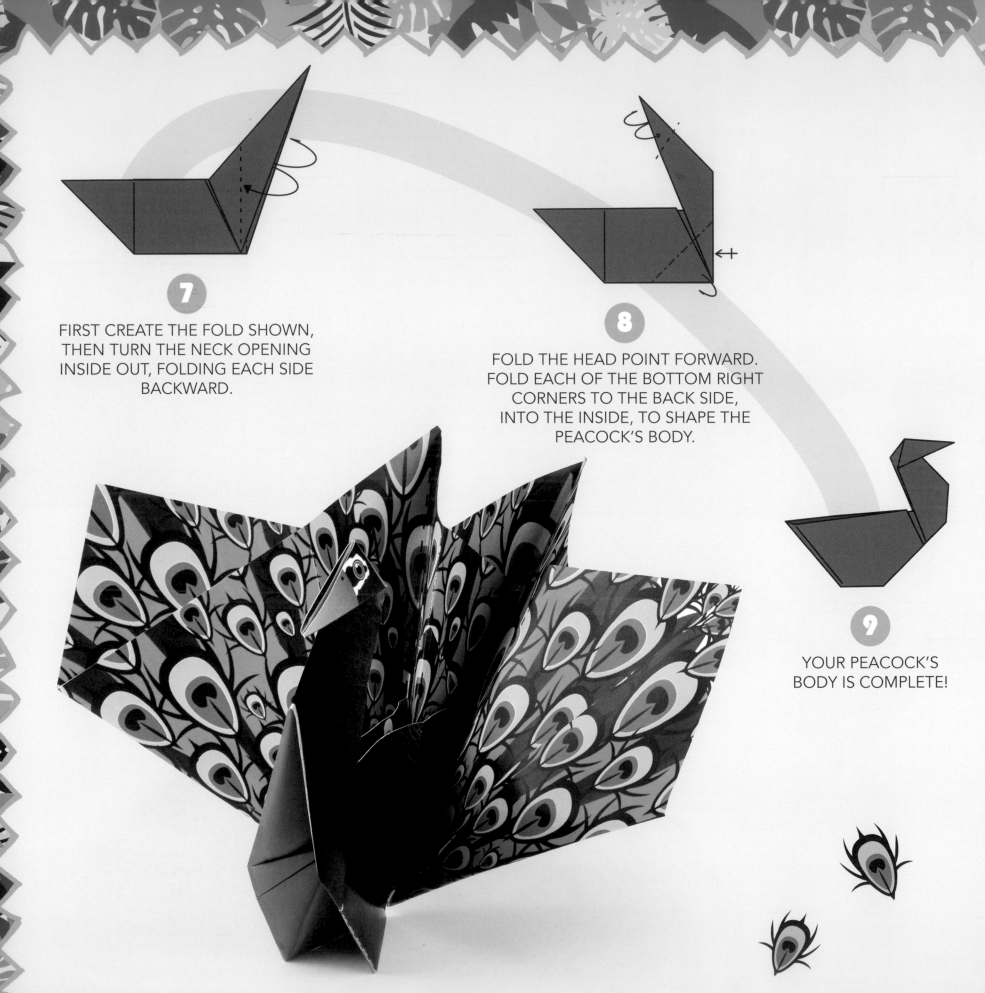

7

FIRST CREATE THE FOLD SHOWN, THEN TURN THE NECK OPENING INSIDE OUT, FOLDING EACH SIDE BACKWARD.

8

FOLD THE HEAD POINT FORWARD. FOLD EACH OF THE BOTTOM RIGHT CORNERS TO THE BACK SIDE, INTO THE INSIDE, TO SHAPE THE PEACOCK'S BODY.

9

YOUR PEACOCK'S BODY IS COMPLETE!

tail

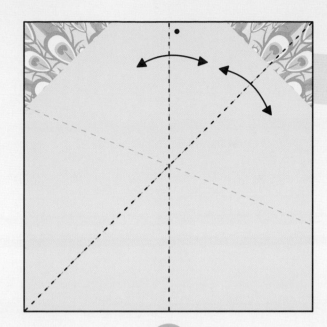

1

FOLD THE SHEET ALONG ONE DIAGONAL AND ONE VERTICAL LINE AS SHOWN, THEN UNFOLD.

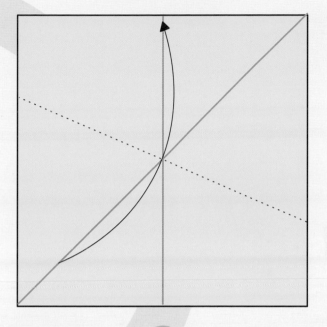

2

FOLD THE SHEET IN TWO, BRINGING THE BOTTOM LEFT CORNER UP TO OVERLAP THE TOP SIDE FOLLOWING THE LINE SHOWN.

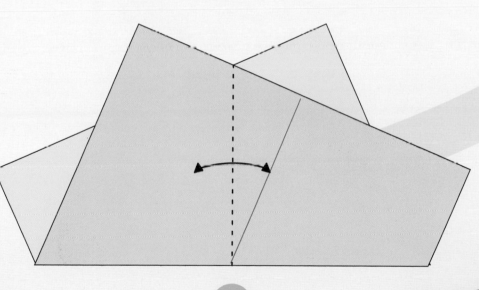

3

FOLD ALONG THE VERTICAL CENTER LINE, THEN UNFOLD.

joining the sections

glue

1

PUT THE CENTRAL TAIL FOLD AGAINST THE REAR OF THE FOLDED BODY AND GLUE THE TWO PARTS TOGETHER. WAIT FOR THE GLUE TO DRY.

2

FOLD IN A ZIGZAG ALONG THE LINES INDICATED, SOMETIMES FOLDING NORMALLY AND SOMETIMES FOLDING TO THE BACK SIDE, FORMING A KIND OF FAN SHAPE.

3

YOUR PEACOCK IS COMPLETE!

finger puppets

Finger puppets are a kind of traditional hand puppet that you wear as if it were a glove on just one finger. Through your hand movements, the characters come to life and show their personalities. You can use them to tell stories. You can imagine conversations between characters and develop stories in your own personal theater!

In this chapter, you will learn how to fold several finger puppets. There is also a special project that you will be able to operate with one whole hand.

Use your puppets to tell a delightful story!

VIDEO: www.nuinui.ch/video/it/L27/simpatici-origamoni/p46

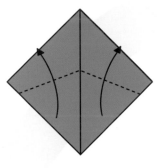

⇧ Sheets included

8 frog

Aesop was a writer in **ancient Greece**. He is said to have invented the literary genre of the fable. In one of his tales, a toad meets an ox. Admiring its large size, the frog tries to grow to become like the ox, but his **attempt fails**! This frog, the first character in our finger puppet collection, is certainly not like that toad. **Starting in the next project**, you'll get to join this frog and a whole host of other animal characters for a **story** that will teach a valuable lesson. But first, fold the frog!

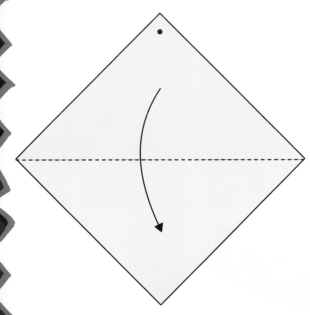

1

FOLD IN HALF ALONG THE HORIZONTAL DIAGONAL LINE, THEN UNFOLD.

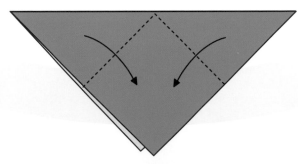

2

FOLD THE TWO OUTER CORNERS DOWN TO MEET THE LOWER CORNER.

DIFFICULTY 1

3

FOLD THE FLAPS UP AS SHOWN SO THAT THE OUTER EDGE OF EACH FLAP IS VERTICAL.

6

NOW WE'LL SHAPE THE EYES. OPEN UP THE TOP FLAPS, FOLDING THEM INSIDE OUT AND DOWN TO FORM TWO SQUARES. SHAPE THE CHEEK WITH A SERIES OF ZIGZAG FOLDS, THEN FOLD THE VERY BOTTOM POINT TO THE BACK SIDE TO FORM THE CHIN.

7

YOUR FROG FINGER PUPPET IS COMPLETE!

5

FLIP THE PIECE OVER.

4

FOLD THE TOP CORNER DOWN. FOLD THE FIRST LAYER OF THE BOTTOM CORNER UP.

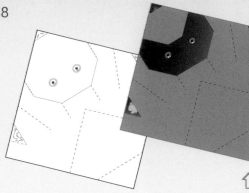

⇧ Sheets included

bear

9

One fine day, while walking along the **banks of a river**, our frog saw a bear. Despite his size, the bear seemed **kind and friendly**. The bear went up to the frog and asked if the frog knew **where birdwatching** was happening. (This story continues in the next project!)

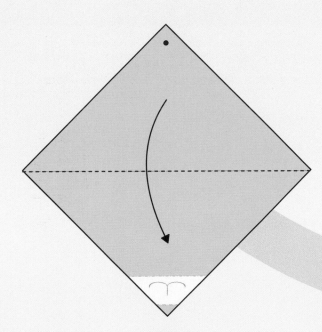

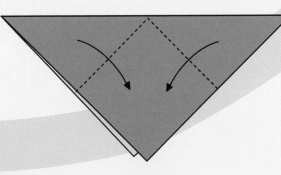

1

FOLD IN HALF ALONG THE HORIZONTAL DIAGONAL LINE.

DIFFICULTY
1

2

FOLD THE TWO OUTER CORNERS IN TO MEET THE BOTTOM CORNER.

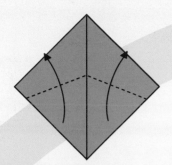

3

FOLD THE FLAPS UP AS SHOWN SO THAT THE OUTER EDGE OF EACH FLAP IS VERTICAL.

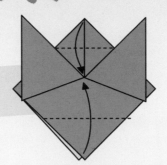

4

FOLD THE FIRST LAYER OF THE BOTTOM FLAP UP TO THE CENTER INTERSECTION. DO THE SAME WITH THE TOP CORNER.

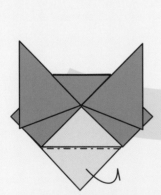

5

FOLD THE SECOND LAYER OF THE BOTTOM FLAP TO THE BACK SIDE. THEN FLIP THE PIECE OVER.

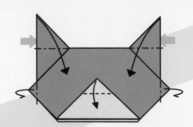

6

FOLD THE CHEEKS TO THE BACK SIDE. FOLD THE NOSE TIP DOWN. FOR THE EARS, OPEN UP THE TOP FLAPS, FOLDING THEM INSIDE OUT AND DOWN TO FORM TWO SQUARES.

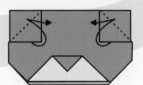

7

TUCK THE SQUARE OF EACH EAR BACK BEHIND THE HEAD.

8

YOUR BEAR FINGER PUPPET
IS COMPLETE!

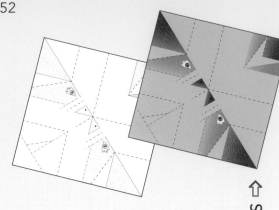

⇧ Sheets included

10 bird

Suddenly, the frog and the bear saw a **bird fly by**, but it was flying too high in the sky. "Look," said the bear. "It's a little bird! How is she **so light and so fast,** and capable of flying to any place she wants? Why am I so **heavy and clumsy** instead? I have to live without leaving the ground. **It's not fair!** Why is that bird able to sing and fly, but I am not?" (This story continues in the next project!)

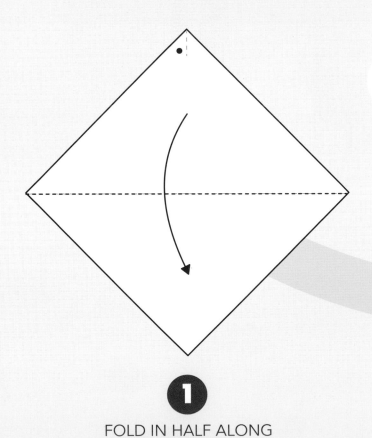

1

FOLD IN HALF ALONG THE HORIZONTAL DIAGONAL LINE.

DIFFICULTY

2

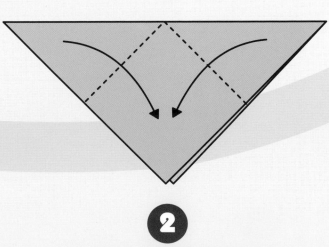

2

FOLD THE TWO OUTER CORNERS IN TO MEET THE BOTTOM CORNER.

52

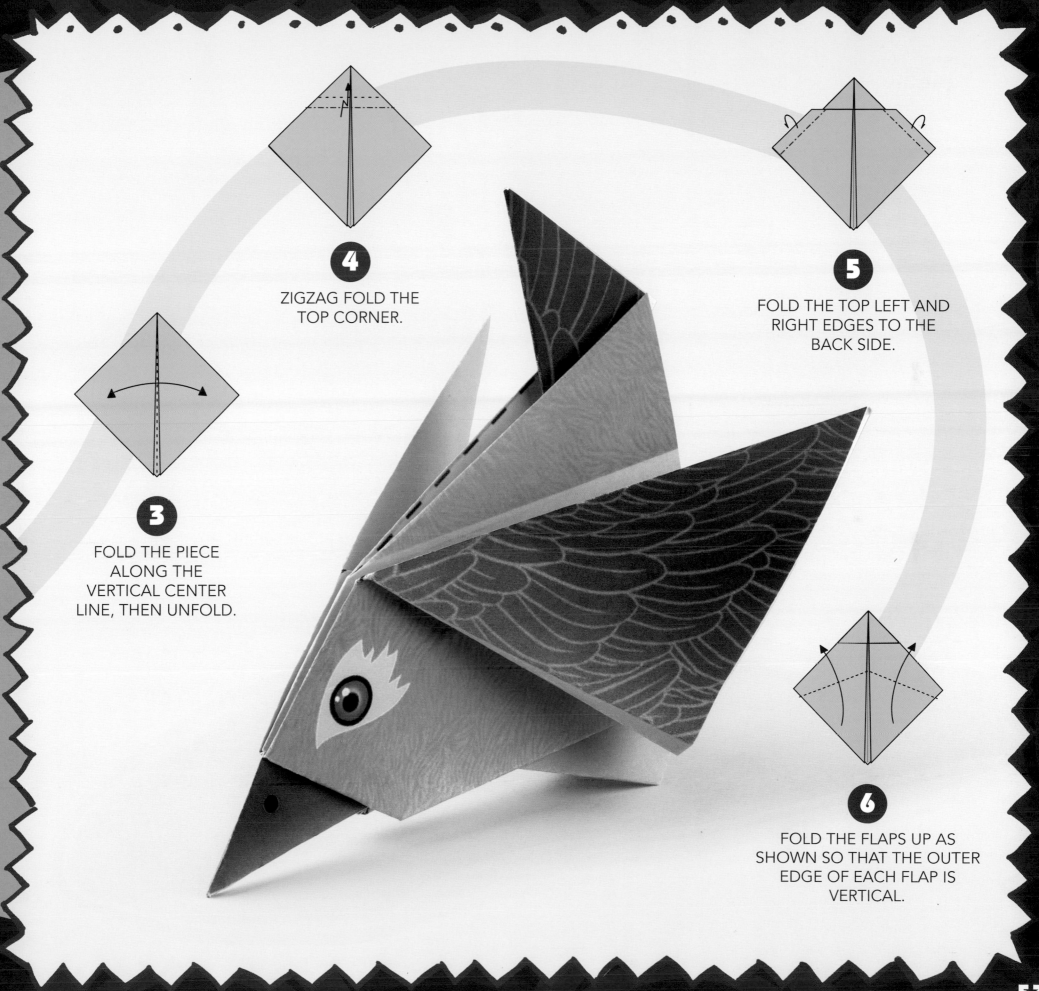

4

ZIGZAG FOLD THE TOP CORNER.

5

FOLD THE TOP LEFT AND RIGHT EDGES TO THE BACK SIDE.

3

FOLD THE PIECE ALONG THE VERTICAL CENTER LINE, THEN UNFOLD.

6

FOLD THE FLAPS UP AS SHOWN SO THAT THE OUTER EDGE OF EACH FLAP IS VERTICAL.

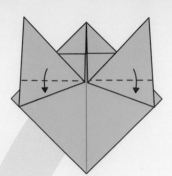

7 FOLD THE FLAPS DOWN ALONG A HORIZONTAL LINE AS SHOWN.

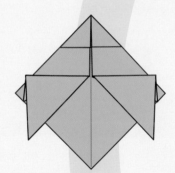

8 FLIP THE PIECE OVER.

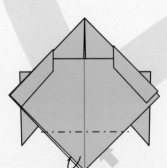

9 FOLD THE FIRST LAYER OF THE BOTTOM CORNER TO THE BACK SIDE.

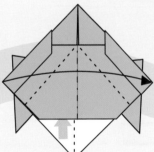

10 FOLD THE PIECE IN HALF FROM LEFT TO RIGHT, PULLING THE FIRST LAYER OF PAPER OF THE CENTER SQUARE UP TO PROTRUDE FORWARD ONCE THE PIECE IS COMPLETELY FOLDED IN HALF.

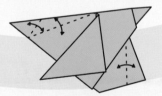

11 BEFORE SHAPING THE TAIL AND NECK, PREPARE THE FOLDS YOU NEED. FOLD AND UNFOLD ALONG THE THREE LINES SHOWN.

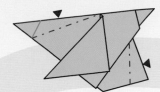

12

USING THE PREVIOUS FOLDS AS GUIDELINES, PUSH THE PAPER INSIDE THE PIECE AT THE EDGES INDICATED BY THE ARROWS (FOLDING THE OUTSIDES IN).

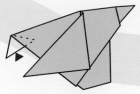

13

FOLD THE TAIL UP, STILL INSIDE/BETWEEN THE FRONT AND BACK OF THE PROJECT.

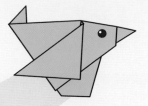

14

YOUR BIRD FINGER PUPPET IS READY!

VIDEO: www.nuinui.ch/video/it/L27/simpatici-origamoni/p56

⇧ Sheets included

11 talking raven

The talking raven, who was resting nearby and had heard every word, said to the frog and the bear, "**Poor little bird!** She lives her entire life fleeing from the hunters who prepare traps to capture her, **lock her in a cage**, and listen to her songs every day. Don't they realize that if you capture a bird, it will be very sad and not want to sing?" "I understand that," said the frog. "I am very **happy to live free in the woods**. I am not jealous of anybody, because I can jump and sing my songs all day long, I always have plenty of food and shelter, and I live happily without any worries." (This story continues in the next project!)

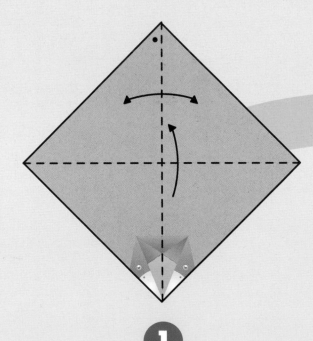

1

FOLD IN HALF ALONG THE DIAGONAL LINES, THEN UNFOLD. FOLD IN HALF UPWARD ALONG THE HORIZONTAL DIAGONAL LINE.

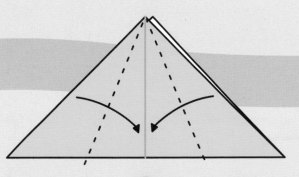

2

FOLD THE OUTER EDGES INWARD TO MEET THE CENTER LINE.

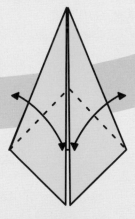

3

FOLD THE BOTTOM CORNERS OUTWARD AS SHOWN.

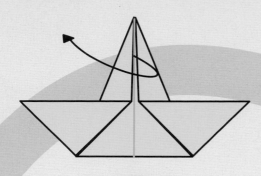

4

PULL THE UPPER LAYER OF PAPER OUT BY BRINGING THE HIDDEN CORNER TO THE SURFACE.

5

FLIP THE PIECE OVER.

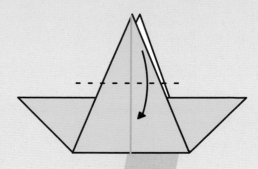

6

FOLD THE FIRST LAYER OF THE TOP CORNER DOWN.

DIFFICULTY
1

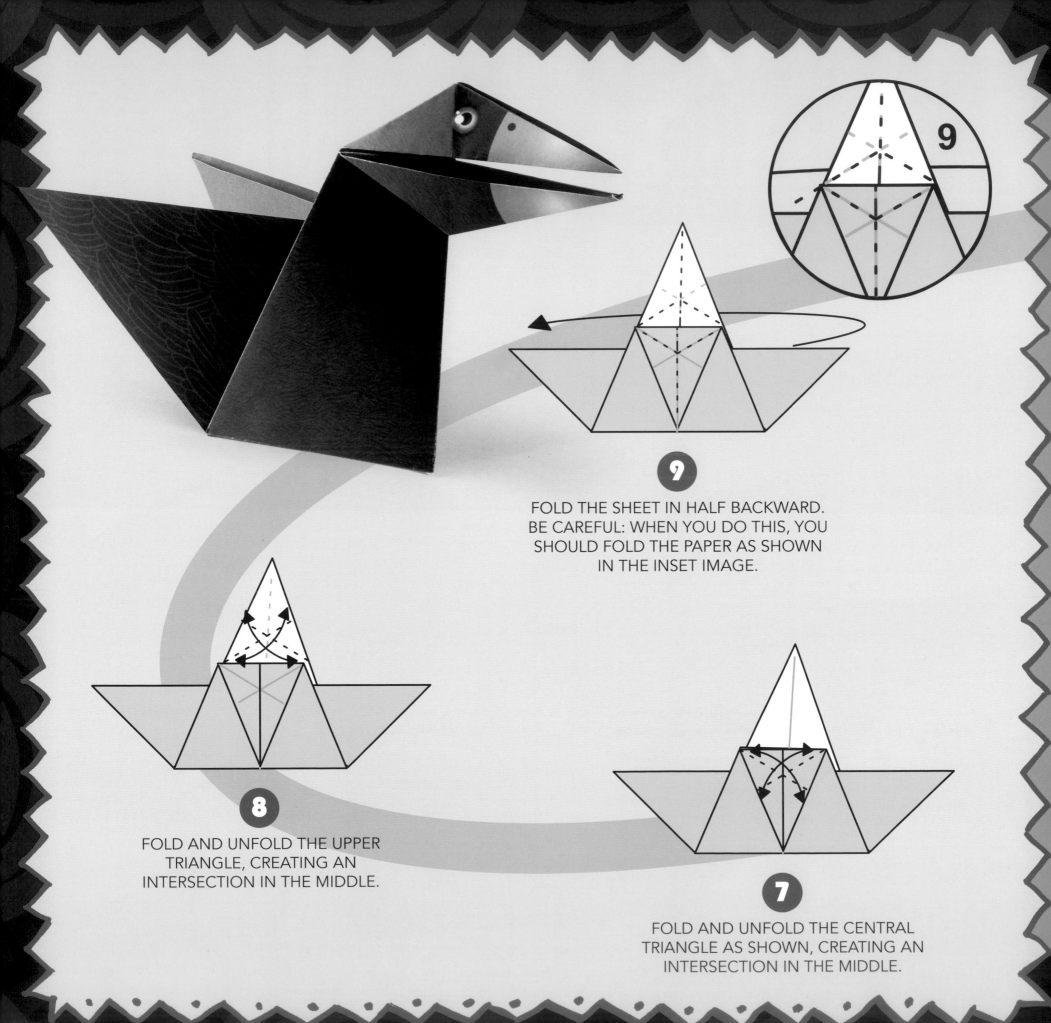

9

FOLD THE SHEET IN HALF BACKWARD.
BE CAREFUL: WHEN YOU DO THIS, YOU
SHOULD FOLD THE PAPER AS SHOWN
IN THE INSET IMAGE.

8

FOLD AND UNFOLD THE UPPER
TRIANGLE, CREATING AN
INTERSECTION IN THE MIDDLE.

7

FOLD AND UNFOLD THE CENTRAL
TRIANGLE AS SHOWN, CREATING AN
INTERSECTION IN THE MIDDLE.

10

YOUR TALKING RAVEN PUPPET IS COMPLETE. MOVE THE FLAPS TO OPEN AND CLOSE THE BEAK!

VIDEO: www.nuinui.ch/video/it/L27/simpatici-origamoni/p60

⇧ Sheets included

12 elephant

Upon hearing this conversation, an **elephant** approached and said, "I would also love to fly like a bird and croak like a frog. And, dear bear, I would really like to have fur like yours! But I don't envy you, I appreciate you. Just like **I admire the little bird for being the way she is.**" Upon hearing this, the bear realized he had good and interesting qualities, too, that he had never noticed before. He **thanked the elephant** for helping him appreciate what he already had, instead of wishing for the things he could not have. Just then, the bird landed on his head and sang a cheerful song! "Don't be sad, bear!" she sang. "**Everyone can be happy for what they already have!**"

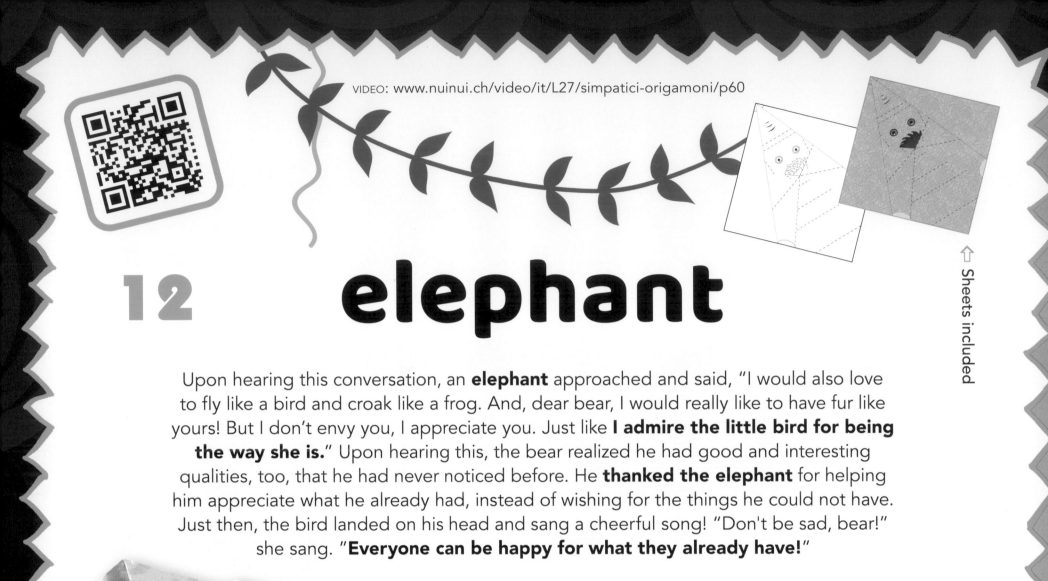

DIFFICULTY

2

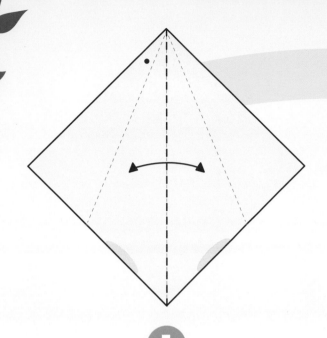

1

FOLD IN HALF ALONG THE
VERTICAL DIAGONAL LINE,
THEN UNFOLD.

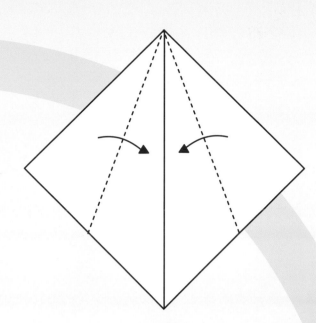

2

FOLD THE SIDES IN
TOWARD THE CENTER
LINE.

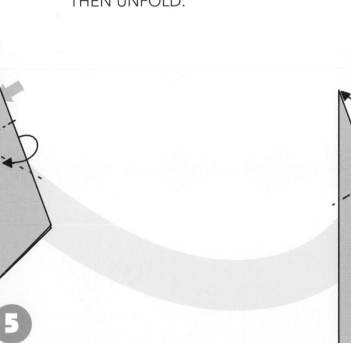

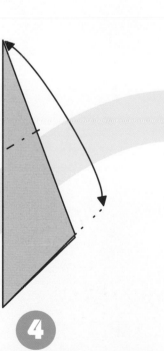

5

USING THE PREVIOUS FOLD AS A
GUIDELINE, OPEN THE PAPER WHERE
THE GRAY ARROW INDICATES AND
PULL IN THE DIRECTION OF THE
BLACK ARROW.

4

FOLD THE TOP CORNER DOWN
AS SHOWN, THEN UNFOLD TO
PREPARE A GUIDELINE TO USE IN
THE NEXT STEP.

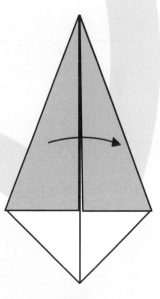

3

FOLD THE PIECE IN
HALF ALONG THE
VERTICAL LINE.

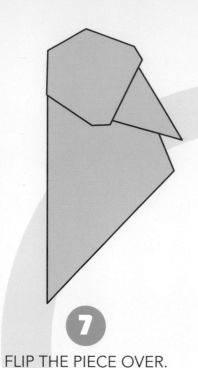

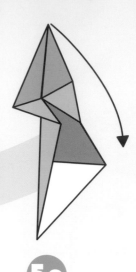

7

FLIP THE PIECE OVER.

6

THE TRIANGLE IS THE HEAD OF THE ELEPHANT. FOLD EACH SIDE TO THE BACK SIDE. FOLD THE TRUNK IN A ZIGZAG.

5a

FOLD THE TOP CORNER DOWNWARD AS SHOWN.

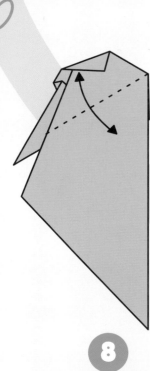

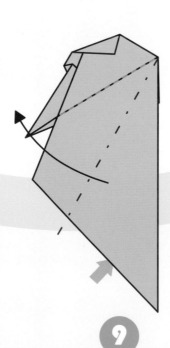

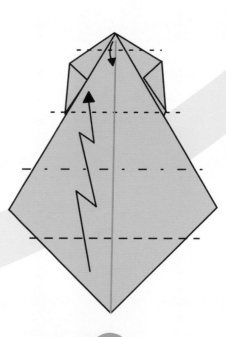

8

FOLD ALONG THE LINE AS SHOWN, THEN UNFOLD.

9

USING THE PREVIOUS FOLD AS A GUIDELINE, OPEN THE PAPER WHERE INDICATED BY THE GRAY ARROW AND PULL IN THE DIRECTION OF THE BLACK ARROW.

10

MAKE A ZIGZAG FOLD FROM THE BOTTOM UP, AND FOLD THE TOP CORNER DOWN.

11

FOLD UP THE TIP OF THE TRUNK. THEN FLIP THE PIECE OVER.

12

YOUR ELEPHANT IS COMPLETE!

children's dreams

These days, many of our wishes involve objects of technology, like cell phones or tablets. But there was a time when childhood had completely different dreams and games. Children used to invent toys out of things they had around the house and the places where they played. Among these toys, for example, were hobby horses made of sticks, dollhouses made of old boxes, and animal puppets made of socks.

I created this set of projects to remind us that in life, we need to have dreams and fantasies, and to make something great out of what's available to us, even if that's just some paper!

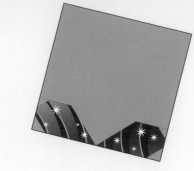

⇧ Sheet included

13 heart badge

To be able to dream, you need to have a **heart**. It is the heart that chooses what we love and desire. Only from the heart does the **energy** develop that leads us to achieve what we want. Therefore, remember that a dream has no meaning if it does not have its **roots in the heart**. This project has a distinctive heart shape, on which you can **draw and write your own dream** to remind you always.

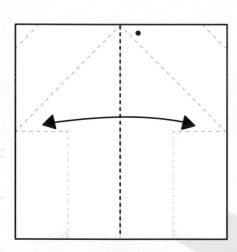

1

FOLD IN HALF ALONG THE VERTICAL CENTER LINE, THEN UNFOLD.

2

FOLD DOWN THE TIPS OF THE TWO TOP CORNERS.

DIFFICULTY
1

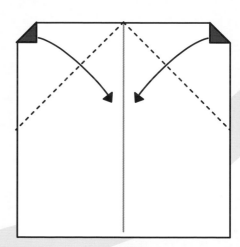

3

FOLD THE TOP CORNERS INTO THE CENTER.

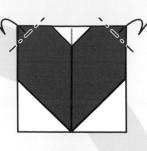

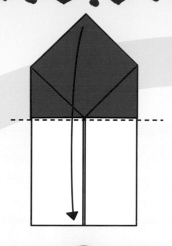

5

FOLD THE PIECE IN HALF DOWNWARD.

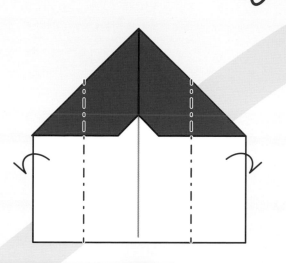

4

FOLD EACH SIDE TO THE BACK SIDE. THEN FLIP THE PIECE OVER.

6

FOLD THE TOP TWO CORNERS TO THE BACK SIDE.

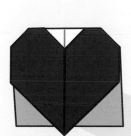

7

YOUR HEART BADGE IS COMPLETE! USE THE PART ON THE BACK OF THE PROJECT TO CARRY IT IN YOUR SHIRT POCKET.

VIDEO: www.nuinui.ch/video/it/L27/simpatici-origamoni/p68

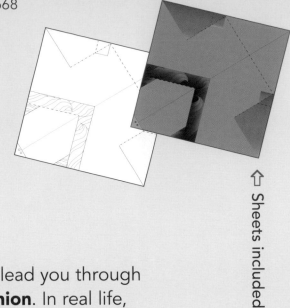

⇧ Sheets included

14

pony

Here is a sweet and beautiful pony—a **tiny horse**—that will lead you through wonderful landscapes and will be your **friend and companion**. In real life, ponies are very small, although they are usually the size of a large dog, not small enough to hold in your hands!

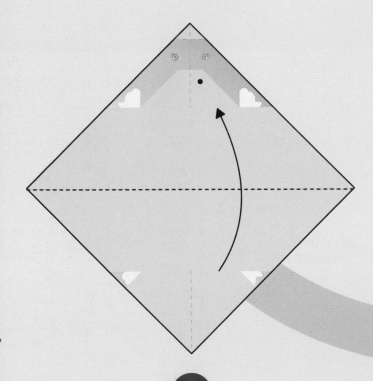

1

FOLD IN HALF ALONG THE HORIZONTAL DIAGONAL LINE, FOLDING UP.

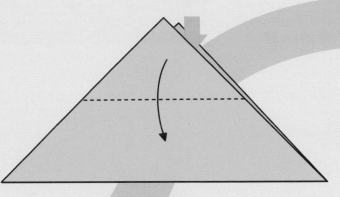

2

FOLD DOWN THE FIRST LAYER OF THE TOP CORNER.

DIFFICULTY

1

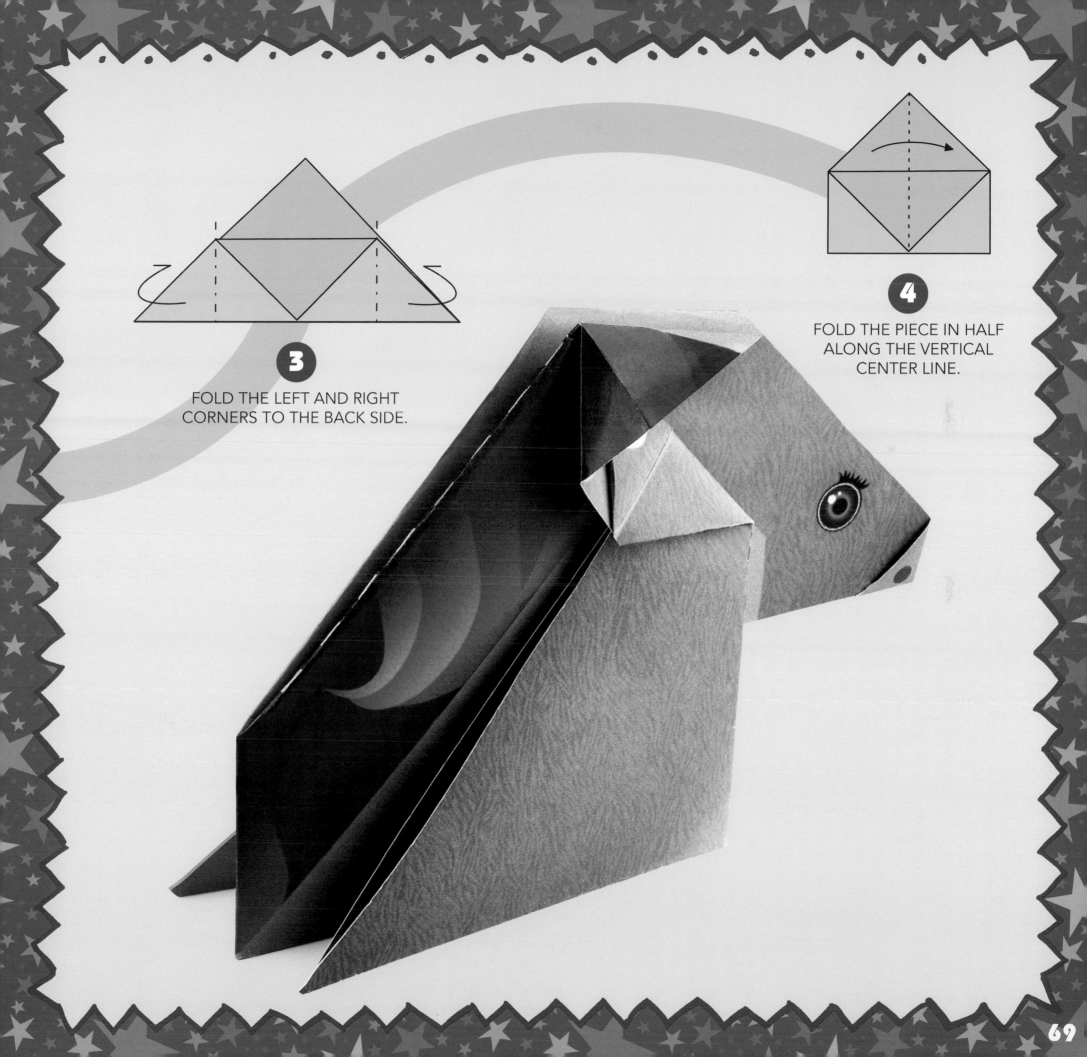

3

FOLD THE LEFT AND RIGHT CORNERS TO THE BACK SIDE.

4

FOLD THE PIECE IN HALF ALONG THE VERTICAL CENTER LINE.

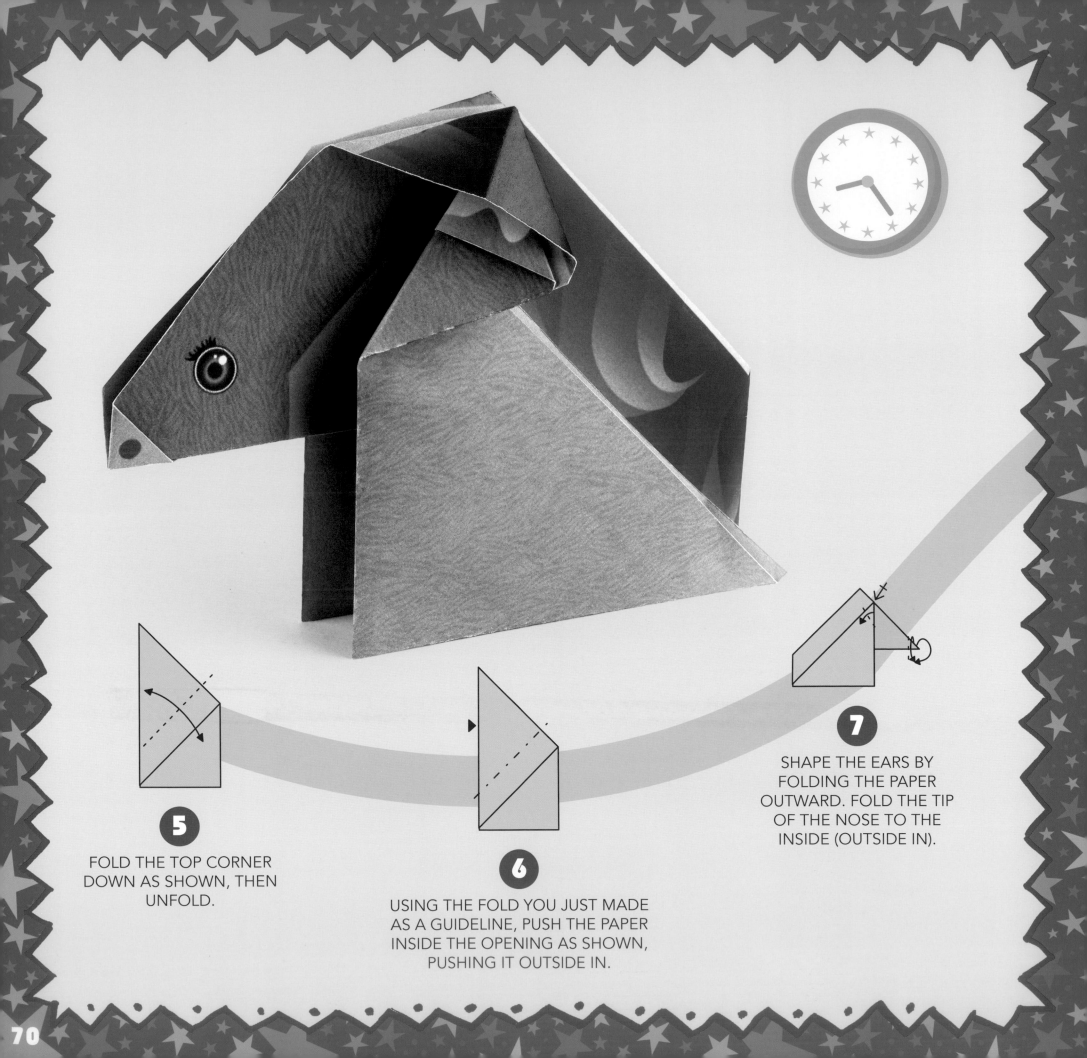

5

FOLD THE TOP CORNER DOWN AS SHOWN, THEN UNFOLD.

6

USING THE FOLD YOU JUST MADE AS A GUIDELINE, PUSH THE PAPER INSIDE THE OPENING AS SHOWN, PUSHING IT OUTSIDE IN.

7

SHAPE THE EARS BY FOLDING THE PAPER OUTWARD. FOLD THE TIP OF THE NOSE TO THE INSIDE (OUTSIDE IN).

8

YOUR PONY IS
COMPLETE!

⇦ Sheet included

15 piano

The piano is a musical instrument that has always created beautiful music. It's like a place of peace where the moment the fingers of the **pianist** begin to touch the **keys**, lovely **harmonious melodies are heard**. A toy piano can encourage the desire to be a real **musician**. The piano should be folded with a sheet of paper of the same size as the Dollhouse Sofa and the Dollhouse Table in order to make sure all the dollhouse furniture is the same size.

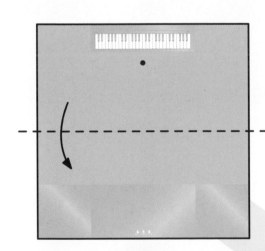

1

FOLD IN HALF ALONG THE HORIZONTAL CENTER LINE.

DIFFICULTY

1

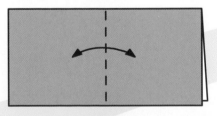

2

FOLD IN HALF, THEN UNFOLD.

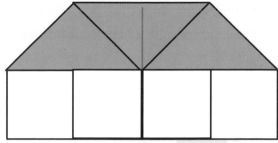

5

HERE IS THE RESULT.

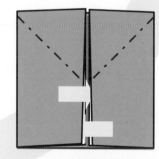

4

PARTIALY UNFOLD THE FLAPS YOU JUST FOLDED AND MANIPULATE AND FLATTEN THE PAPER TO FORM A KIND OF ROOF SHAPE.

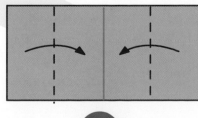

3

FOLD EACH EDGE INTO THE CENTER LINE.

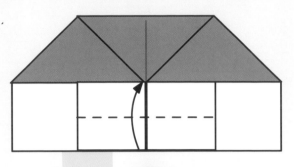

6

FOLD THE FIRST LAYER OF
THE BOTTOM MIDDLE UP
TO THE CENTER.

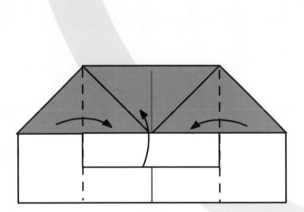

7

FOLD THE SIDES IN TO BE
PERPENDICULAR TO THE FLAT
BACK OF THE PIANO. LIFT AND
PULL THE KEYBOARD TO CREATE
THE FINAL SHAPE OF THE PIANO.

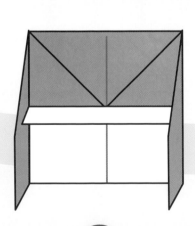

8

YOUR PIANO IS COMPLETE!

VIDEO: www.nuinui.ch/video/it/L27/simpatici-origamoni/p76

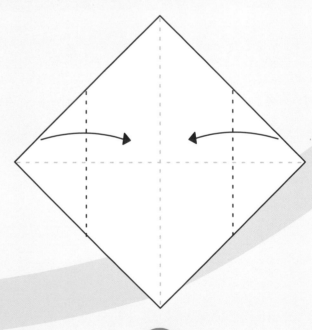

↪ Sheets included

16 teddy bear

Stuffed **teddy bears** are cute and loveable toys. We call them teddy bears as a reference to **Theodore Roosevelt**, the 26th president of the United States of America. "Teddy" is a nickname for Theodore. During a hunting trip, the president **decided not to shoot a bear** he saw. From then on, stuffed bears became known as teddy bears. This origami project forms the body of a teddy bear—add the Bear finger puppet project to it as the head!

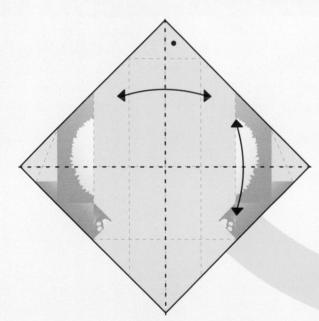

DIFFICULTY

1

1

FOLD IN HALF ALONG THE DIAGONAL LINES, THEN UNFOLD.

2

FOLD THE SIDE CORNERS TO THE CENTER.

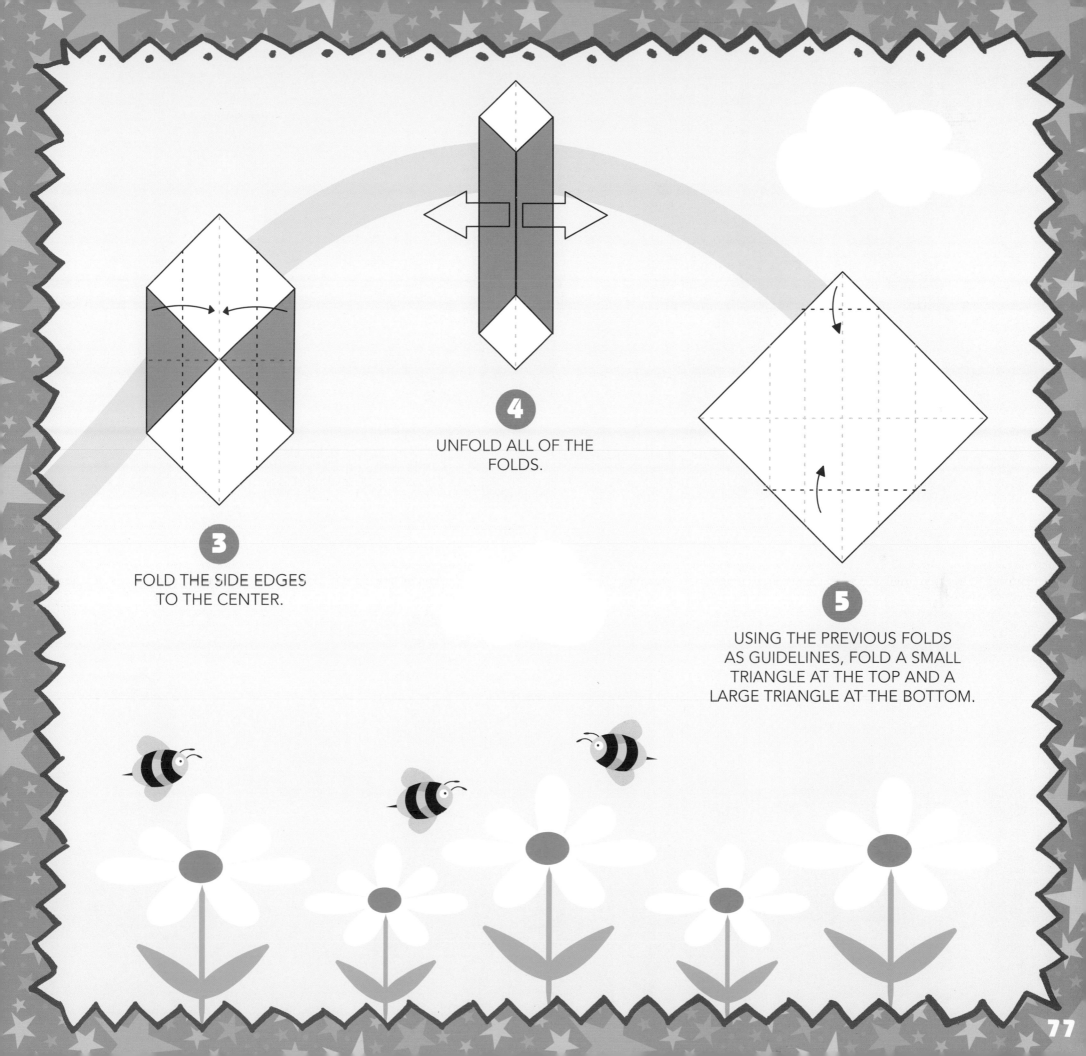

3

FOLD THE SIDE EDGES
TO THE CENTER.

4

UNFOLD ALL OF THE
FOLDS.

5

USING THE PREVIOUS FOLDS
AS GUIDELINES, FOLD A SMALL
TRIANGLE AT THE TOP AND A
LARGE TRIANGLE AT THE BOTTOM.

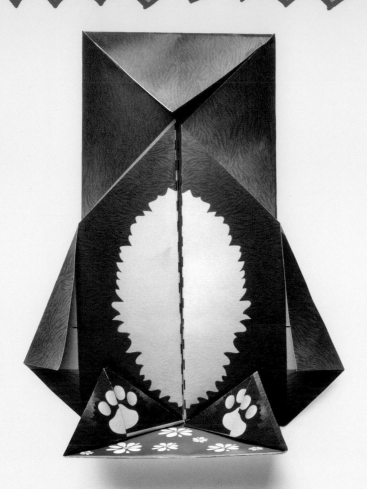

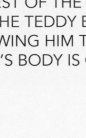

8

FOLD THE BOTTOM RECTANGULAR SECTION UP SO IT IS PERPENDICULAR TO THE FLAT REST OF THE PAPER. THESE ARE THE TEDDY BEAR'S FEET, ALLOWING HIM TO SIT. YOUR BEAR'S BODY IS COMPLETE!

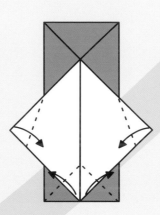

7

FOLD THE BOTTOM TWO FLAPS FROM THE CENTER TO THE OUTSIDE. TO FORM THE ARMS, FOLD THE SIDE CORNERS DOWN AS SHOWN.

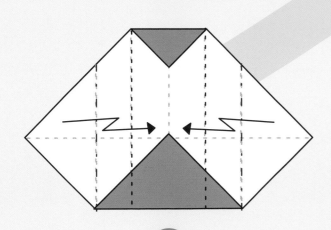

6

USING THE PREVIOUS FOLDS AS GUIDELINES, FOLD A ZIGZAG AS SHOWN.

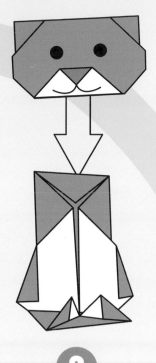

9

PUT THE HEAD OF THE BEAR (FINGER PUPPET PROJECT 9) ONTO THE BODY AS SHOWN. YOUR TEDDY BEAR IS COMPLETE!

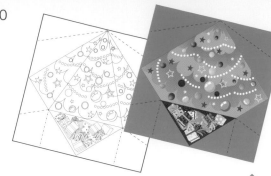

⇧ Sheets included

17 Christmas tree

Many childhood dreams and memories are related to Christmas and the winter holidays. During this period, people are usually more **generous** and will exchange greetings with friends and relatives. Many families also set up a Christmas tree and **exchange gifts**. This is why I created the project of the Christmas tree in origami. This is a great project to customize. You can draw on it or glue photos or glitter to it . . . I'll leave it to your creativity!

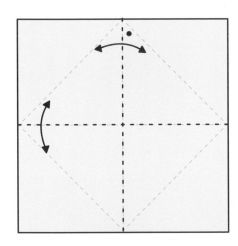

1

FOLD IN HALF ALONG THE HORIZONTAL AND VERTICAL LINES, THEN UNFOLD.

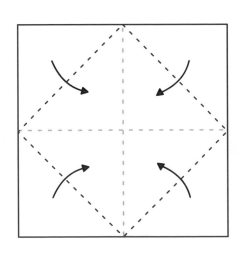

2

FOLD THE CORNERS INTO THE CENTER.

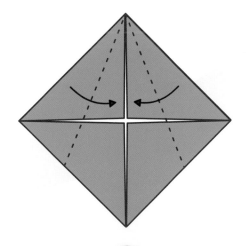

3

FOLD THE TOP SIDES TO THE CENTER LINE.

DIFFICULTY
1

80

4

FOLD THE BASE OF
THE TREE TO THE
BACK SIDE.

5

YOUR CHRISTMAS TREE
IS COMPLETE!

VIDEO: www.nuinui.ch/video/it/L27/simpatici-origamoni/p82

Christmas ornament

18

⇦ Sheets included

There are many different types of Christmas tree **decorations**. This one is simple. You can make it in many bright colors. Once you have folded it, make a small hole at the top and **insert a hook to hang it**, with the help of an adult. Liven up your Christmas tree or dinner table with these vibrant decorations!

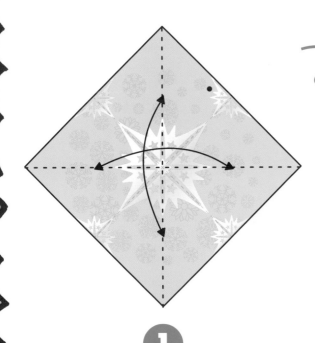

1

FOLD IN HALF ALONG THE DIAGONAL LINES, THEN UNFOLD. FLIP THE PIECE OVER.

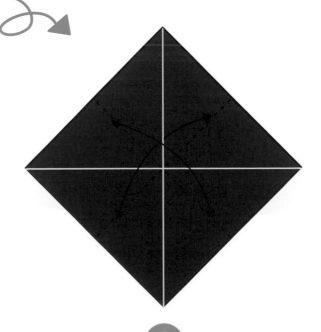

2

FOLD IN HALF ALONG THE HORIZONTAL AND VERTICAL CENTER LINES, THEN UNFOLD.

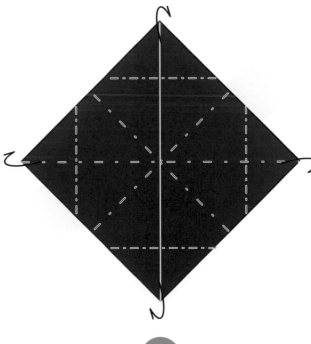

3

FOLD ALL FOUR CORNERS TO THE BACK SIDE.

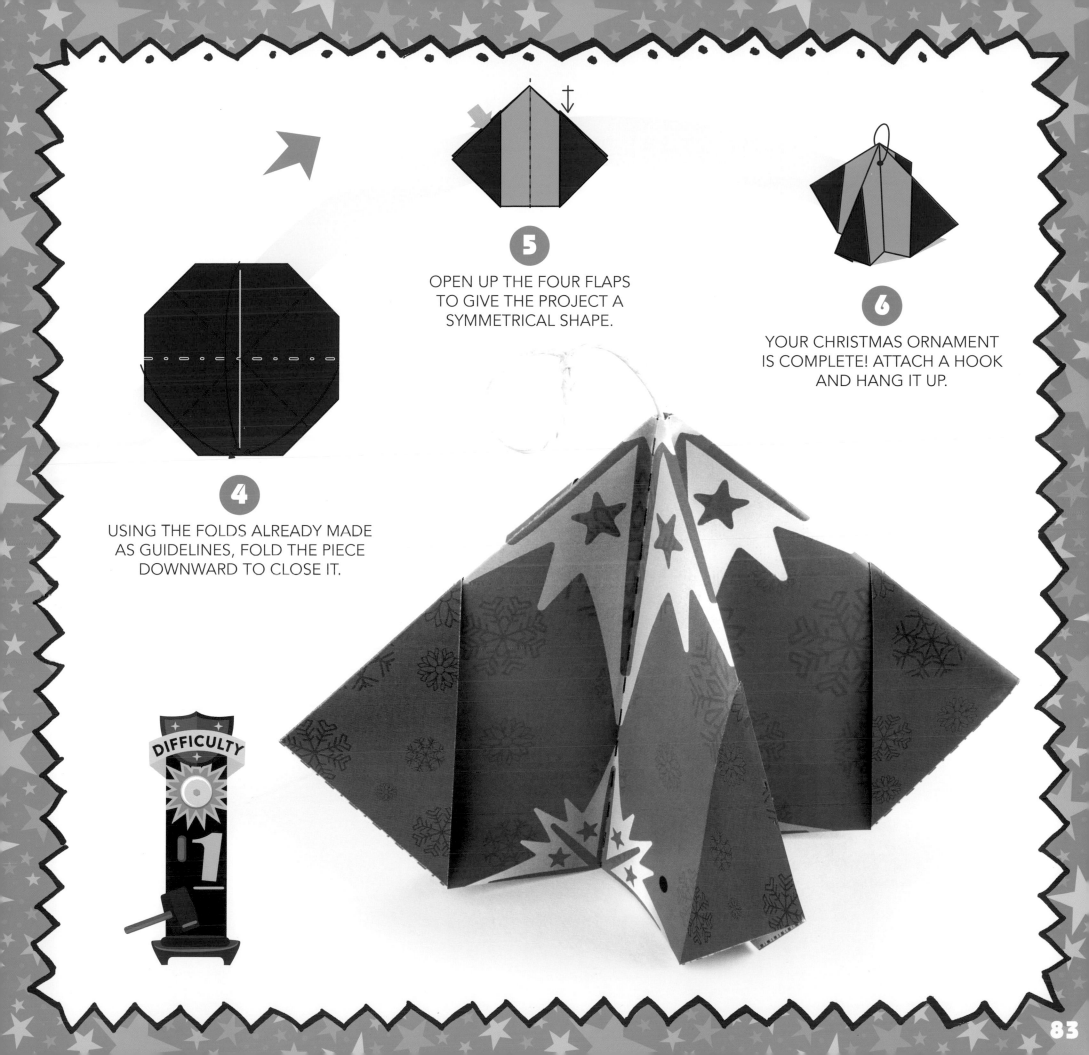

5

OPEN UP THE FOUR FLAPS
TO GIVE THE PROJECT A
SYMMETRICAL SHAPE.

6

YOUR CHRISTMAS ORNAMENT
IS COMPLETE! ATTACH A HOOK
AND HANG IT UP.

4

USING THE FOLDS ALREADY MADE
AS GUIDELINES, FOLD THE PIECE
DOWNWARD TO CLOSE IT.

DIFFICULTY

1

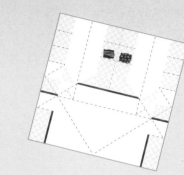

⇧ Sheet included

19 dollhouse sofa

Dollhouses are environments for children that are enchanted and full of fantasy. I created this sofa with the idea of making a **cute little living room**. The project folding starts like the instructions for the Piano. The sofa should be folded with a sheet of paper of the same size as the Piano and the Dollhouse Table in order to make sure all the dollhouse furniture is the same size.

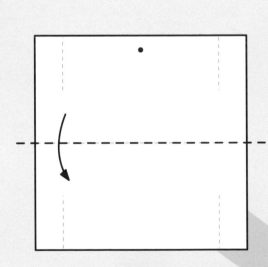

1

FOLD IN HALF ALONG THE HORIZONTAL CENTER LINE.

DIFFICULTY **3**

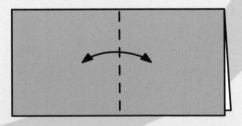

2

FOLD IN HALF, THEN UNFOLD.

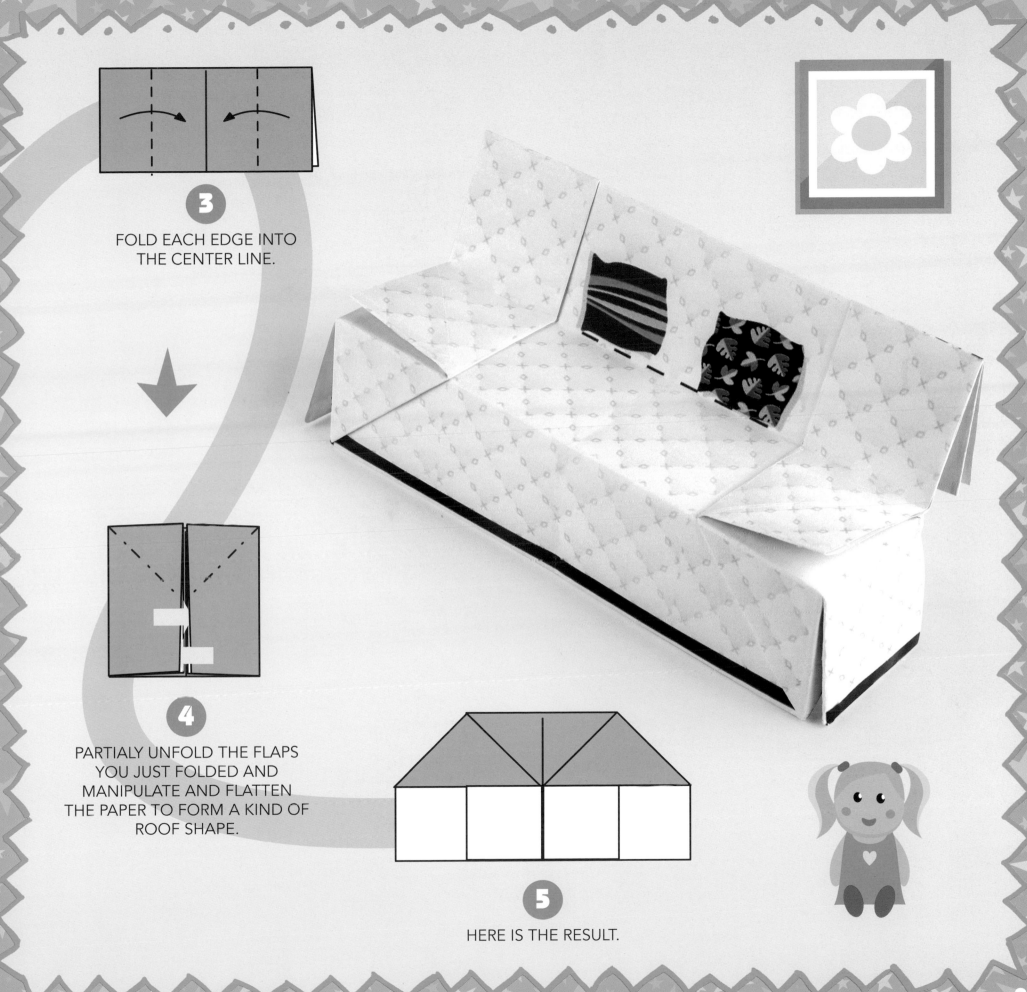

3

FOLD EACH EDGE INTO THE CENTER LINE.

4

PARTIALY UNFOLD THE FLAPS YOU JUST FOLDED AND MANIPULATE AND FLATTEN THE PAPER TO FORM A KIND OF ROOF SHAPE.

5

HERE IS THE RESULT.

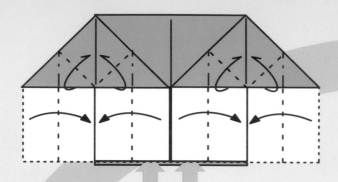

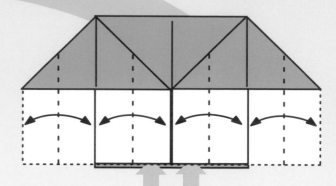

7

FOLD THE FOUR FLAPS IN HALF AGAIN, BUT AT THE SAME TIME, FOLD THE CENTER OF THE PAPER IN TWO SPOTS BY RAISING IT AS SHOWN WITH THE ARROWS.

6

FOLD EACH OF THE FOUR FLAPS IN HALF, THEN UNFOLD.

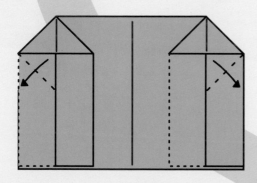

8

FOLD THE CORNERS OF THE OUTER FLAPS DOWN.

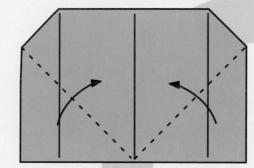

10

FOLD EACH LOWER EDGE INTO THE CENTER LINE.

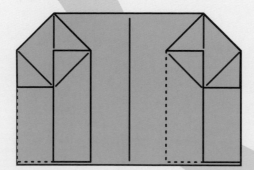

9

FLIP THE PIECE OVER.

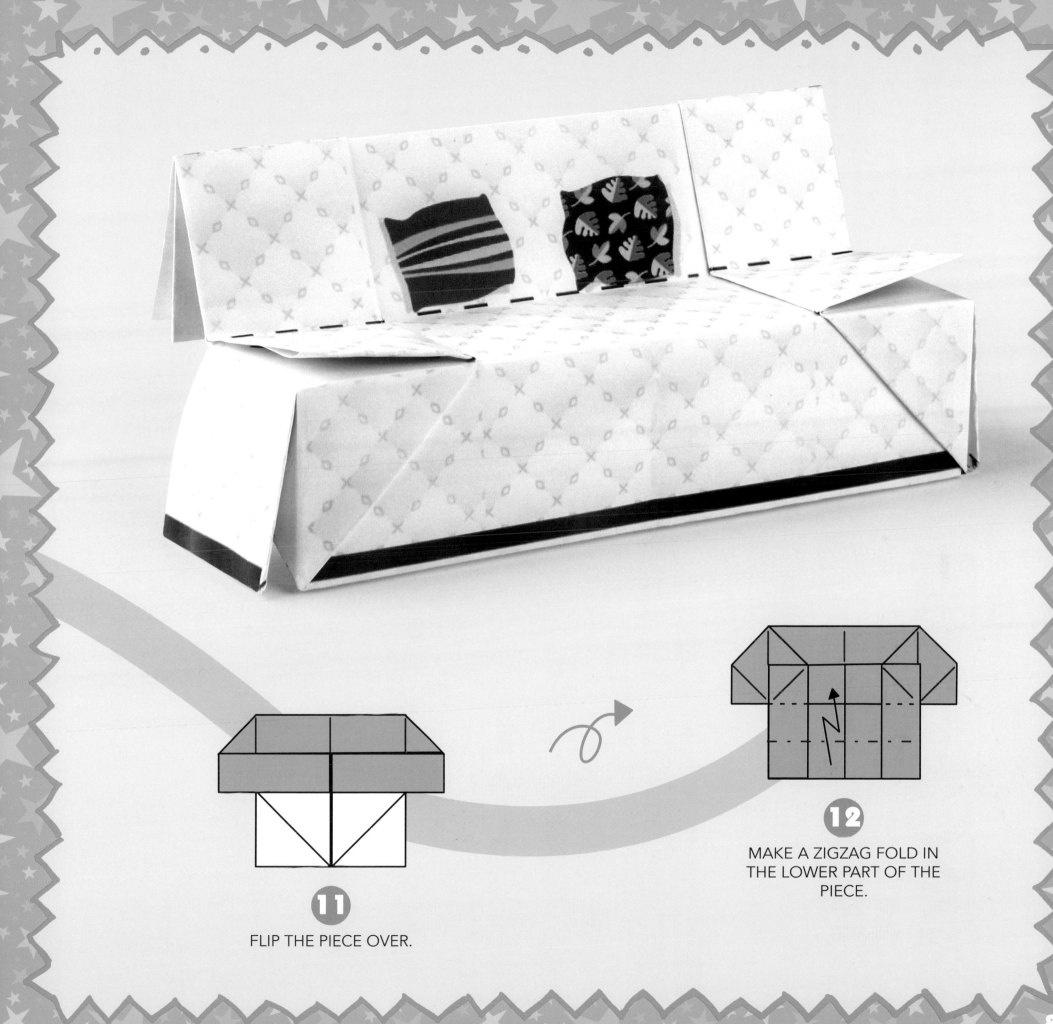

11

FLIP THE PIECE OVER.

12

MAKE A ZIGZAG FOLD IN THE LOWER PART OF THE PIECE.

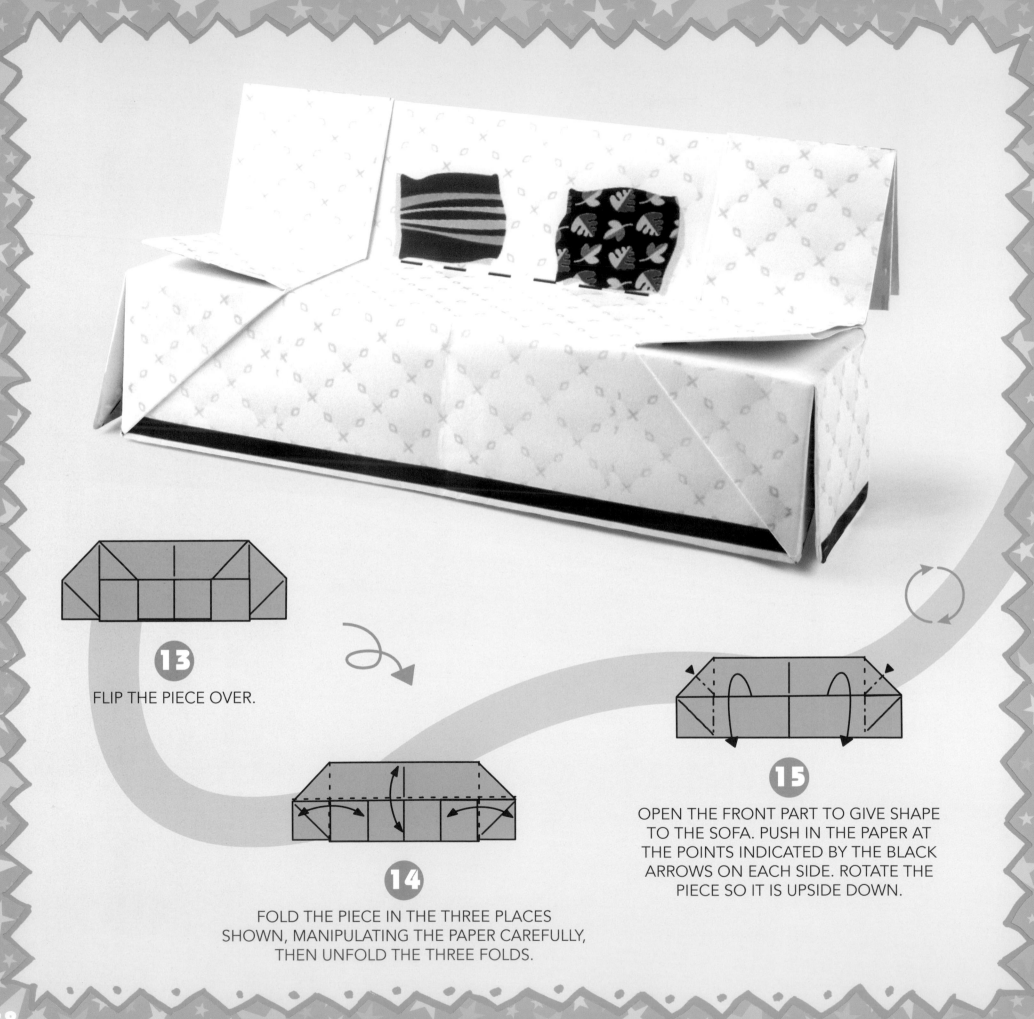

13

FLIP THE PIECE OVER.

14

FOLD THE PIECE IN THE THREE PLACES
SHOWN, MANIPULATING THE PAPER CAREFULLY,
THEN UNFOLD THE THREE FOLDS.

15

OPEN THE FRONT PART TO GIVE SHAPE
TO THE SOFA. PUSH IN THE PAPER AT
THE POINTS INDICATED BY THE BLACK
ARROWS ON EACH SIDE. ROTATE THE
PIECE SO IT IS UPSIDE DOWN.

16

YOUR DOLLHOUSE SOFA IS READY!

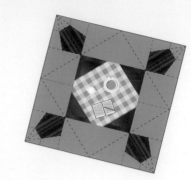

⇧ Sheet included

20 dollhouse table

Here is the **dollhouse table**, which can be part of the living room or even the bedroom. Thanks to this table, your dolls can **visit with their friends**, and you get to **invent** this part of the story! The table should be folded with a sheet of paper of the same size as the Piano and the Dollhouse Sofa in order to make sure all the dollhouse furniture is the same size.

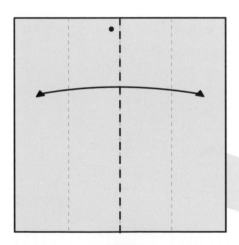

1

FOLD IN HALF ALONG
THE VERTICAL CENTER
LINE, THEN UNFOLD.

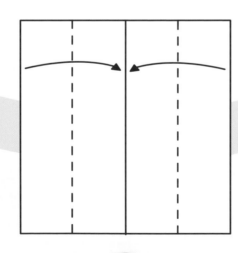

2

FOLD EACH SIDE IN TO MEET
THE CENTER LINE.

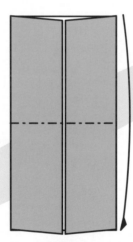

3

FOLD THE PIECE IN HALF
TO THE BACK SIDE.

DIFFICULTY
3

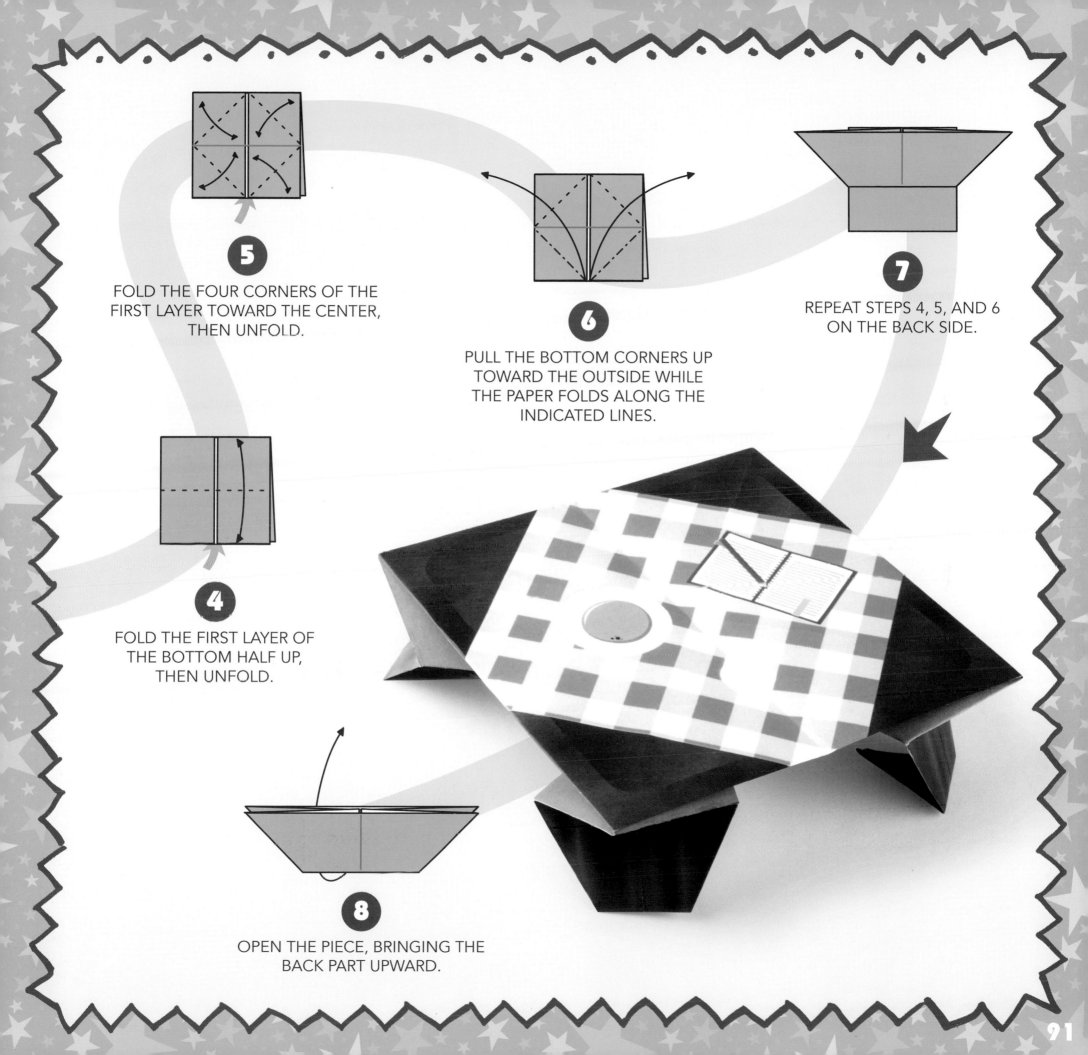

5

FOLD THE FOUR CORNERS OF THE FIRST LAYER TOWARD THE CENTER, THEN UNFOLD.

6

PULL THE BOTTOM CORNERS UP TOWARD THE OUTSIDE WHILE THE PAPER FOLDS ALONG THE INDICATED LINES.

7

REPEAT STEPS 4, 5, AND 6 ON THE BACK SIDE.

4

FOLD THE FIRST LAYER OF THE BOTTOM HALF UP, THEN UNFOLD.

8

OPEN THE PIECE, BRINGING THE BACK PART UPWARD.

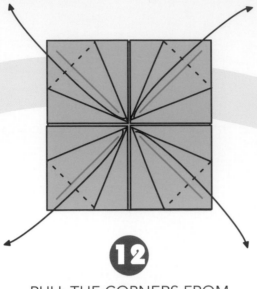

12

PULL THE CORNERS FROM
THE CENTER TO THE OUTSIDE.
THE PAPER WILL FOLD USING
THE FOLDS MADE IN THE
PREVIOUS STEPS.

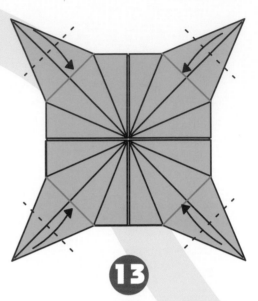

13

FOLD THE CORNERS INWARD.

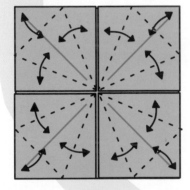

11

FOLD AND UNFOLD TO FORM
THE FOLDS INDICATED ON
ALL OF THE UPPER SQUARES.

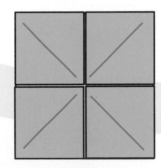

10

HERE IS THE RESULT.

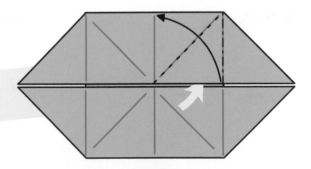

9

LIFTING THE PAPER WHERE INDICATED
BY THE GRAY ARROW, MAKE THE TWO
FOLDS AS SHOWN. REPEAT IN THE
OTHER THREE CORNERS.

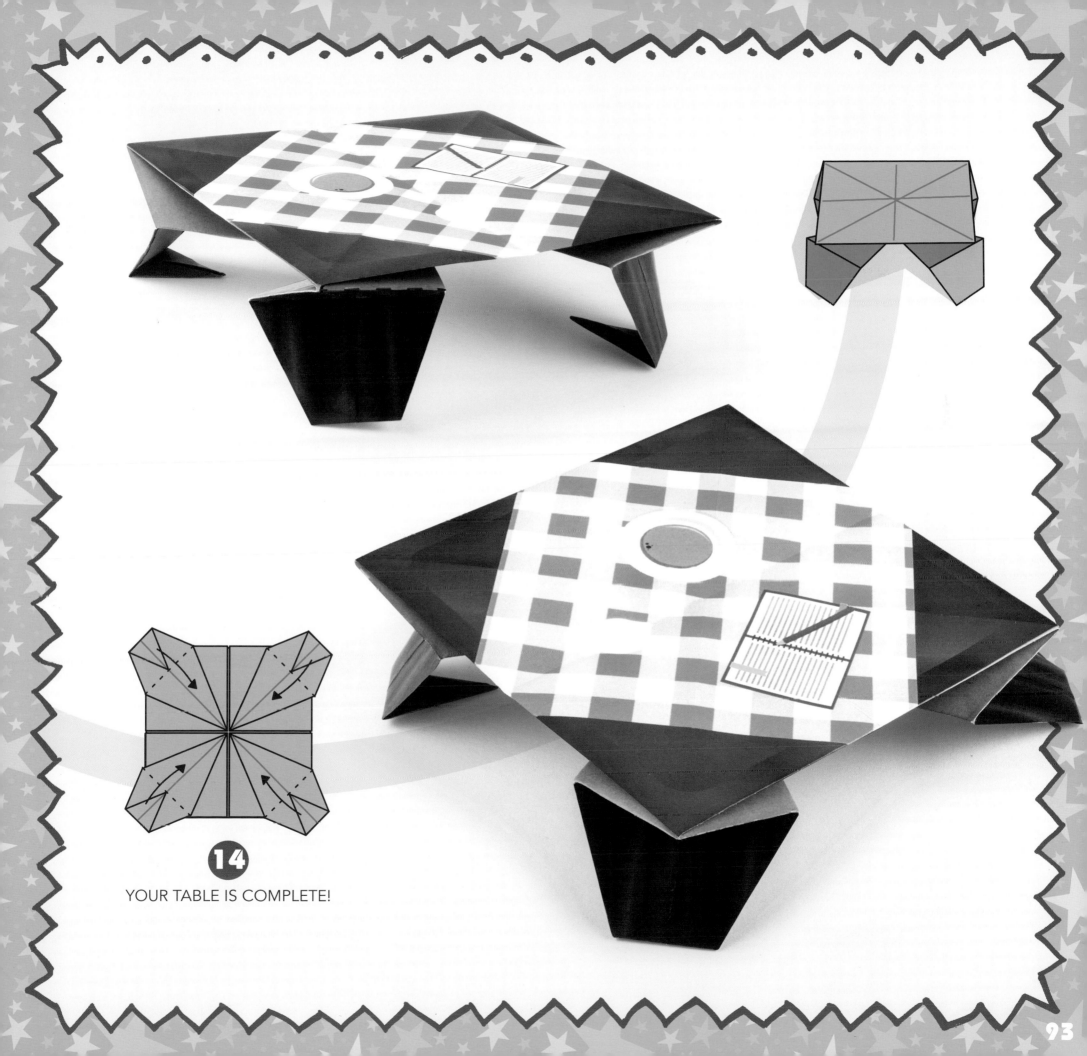

14

YOUR TABLE IS COMPLETE!

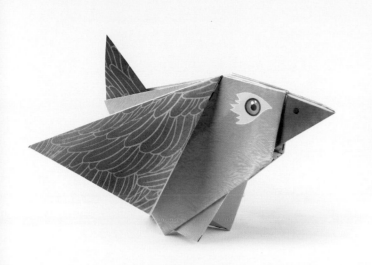

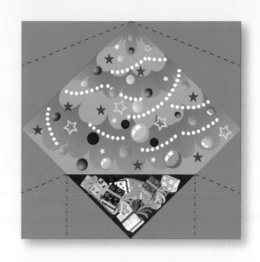

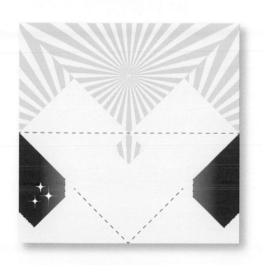

A simple sheet of paper transforms like magic . . .

Rita Foelker, a writer and journalist with a master's degree in philosophy, is also, and above all, a mother. Born in Brazil, where she lives and works in the field of publishing as an author and illustrator, she has been studying and teaching the ancient Japanese art of origami since 1987 and has participated in various international projects. Her origami creations have been published in many countries, including in the journal of the prestigious British Origami Society. Author of numerous volumes of origami published in Brazil, she has created several books, including *Magic Origami*, *The Origami Garden*, *The Origami Galaxy*, *Relaxing Origami Mandalas*, and *Awesome Origami*. Visit her at her website: **http://rfoelker.wix.com/superorigami**

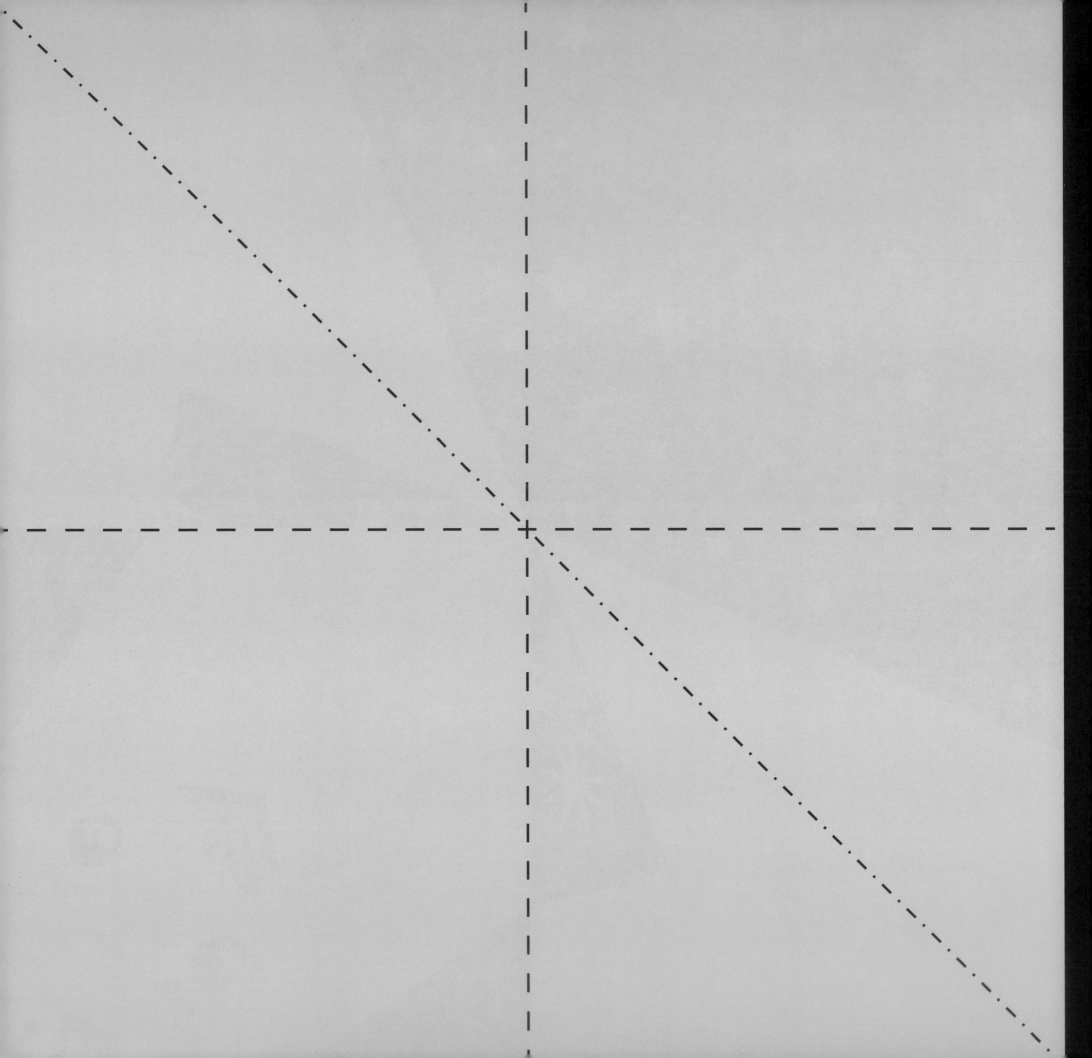

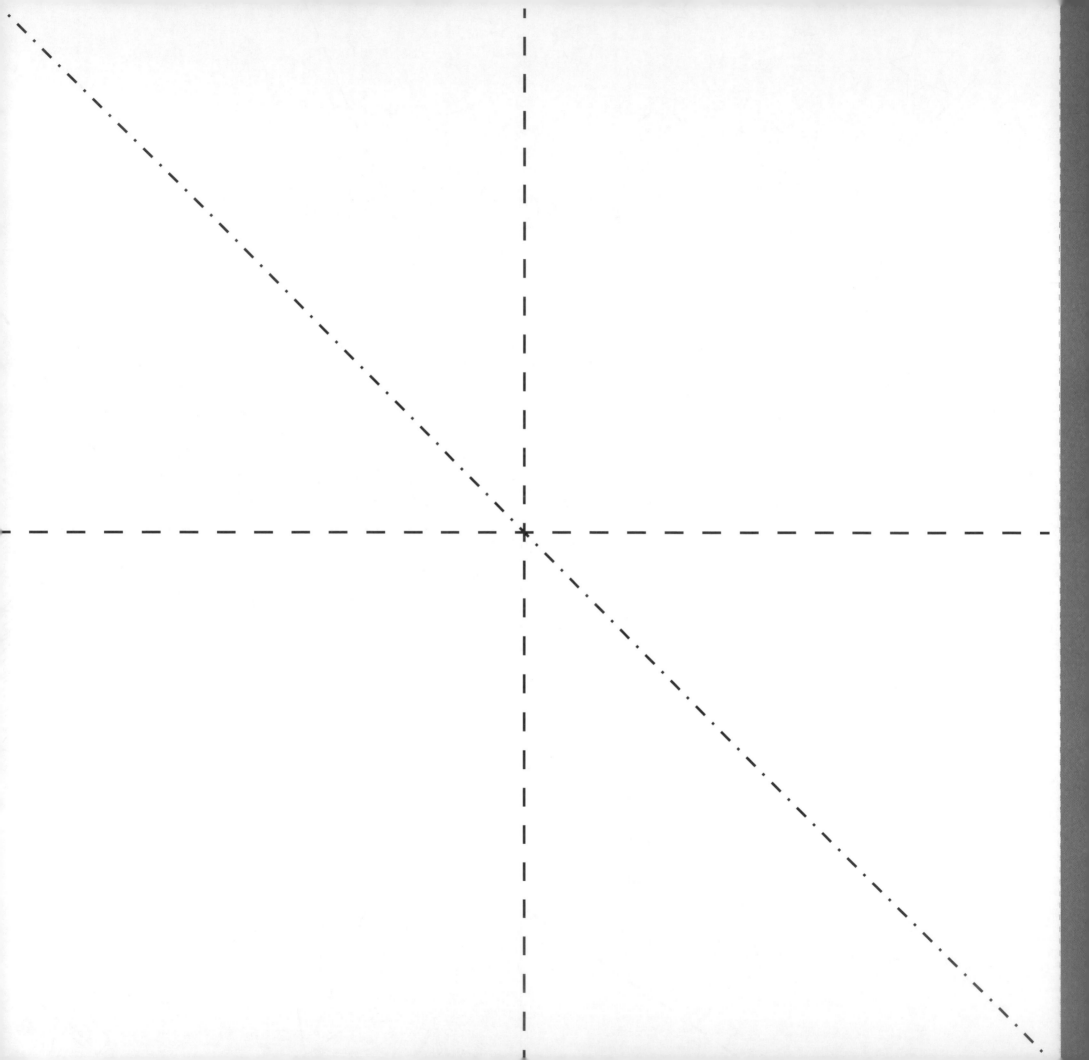

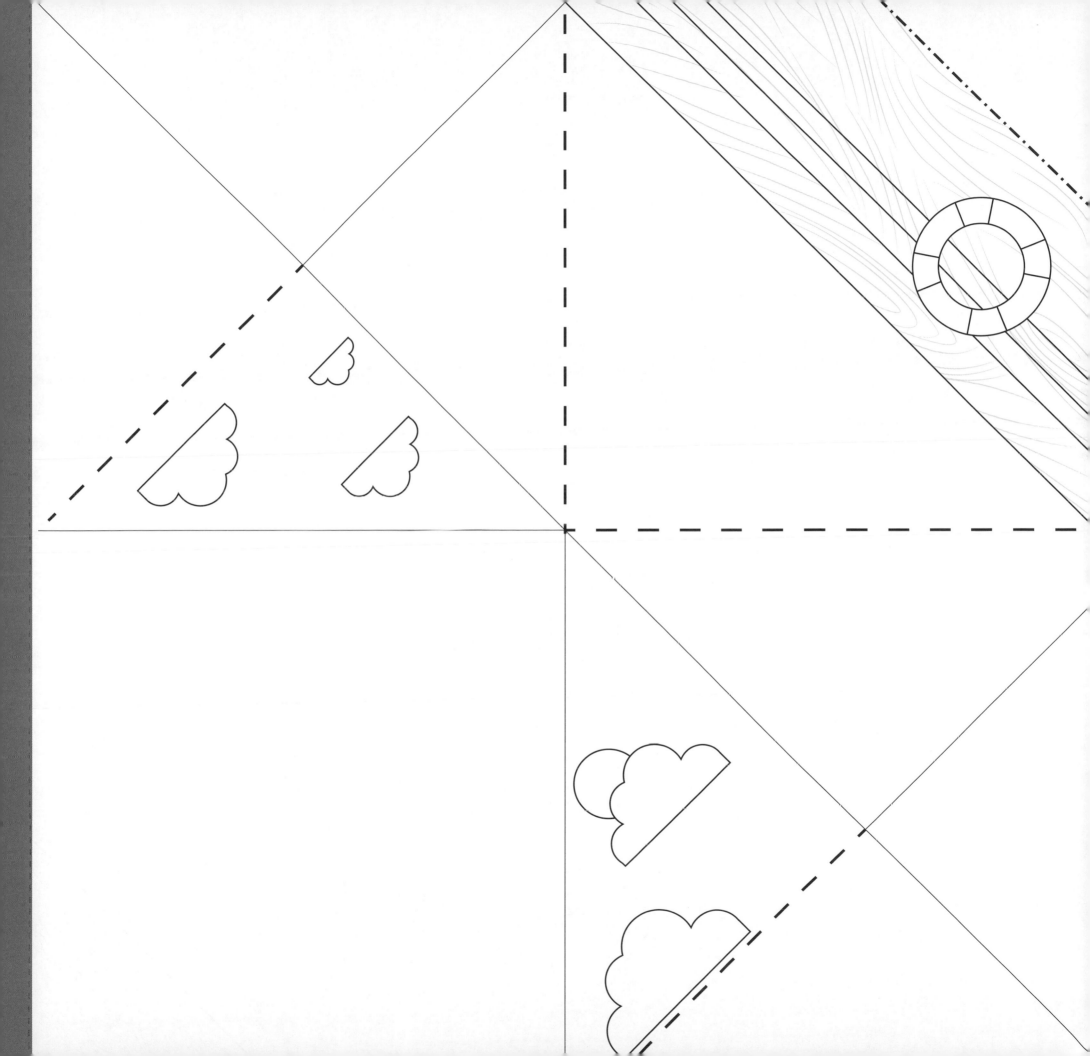

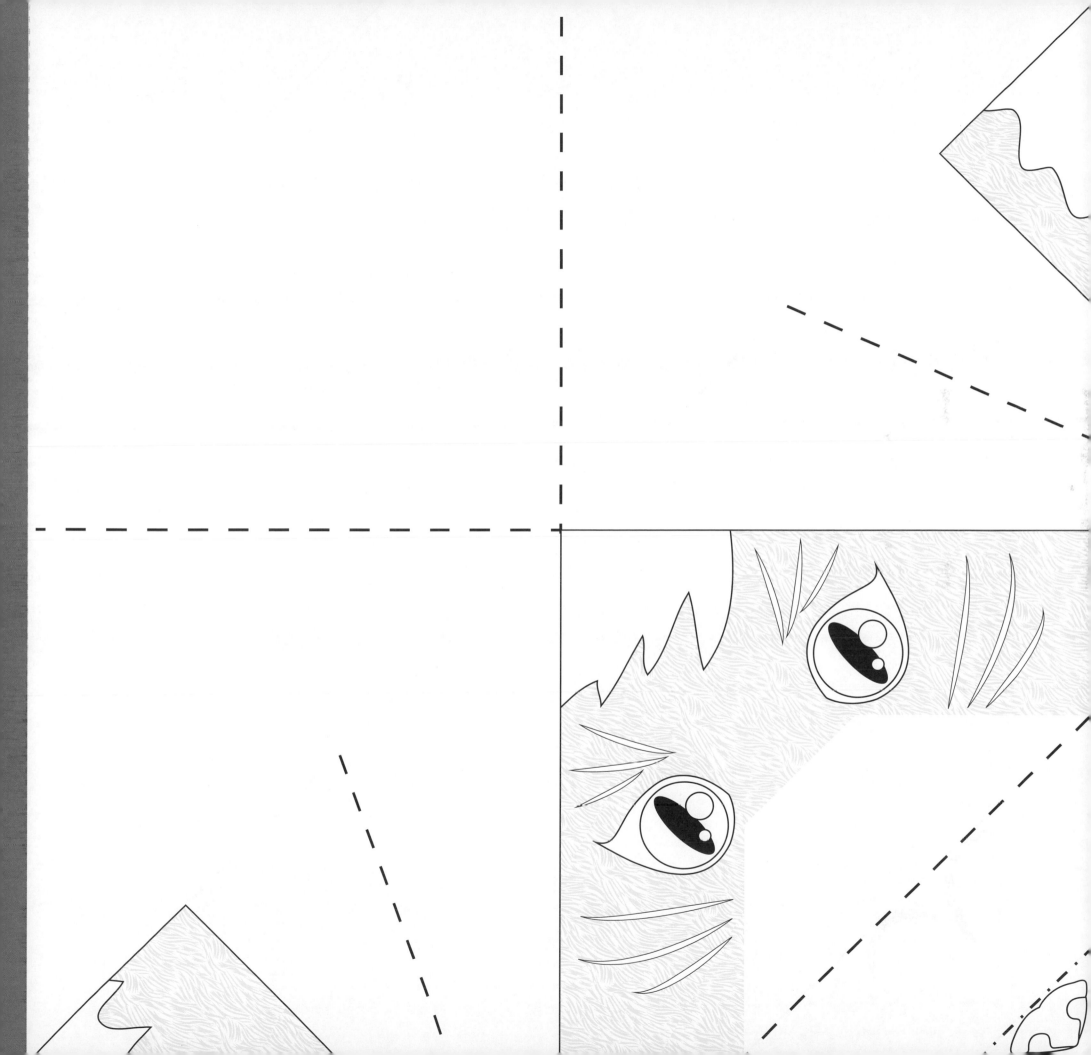

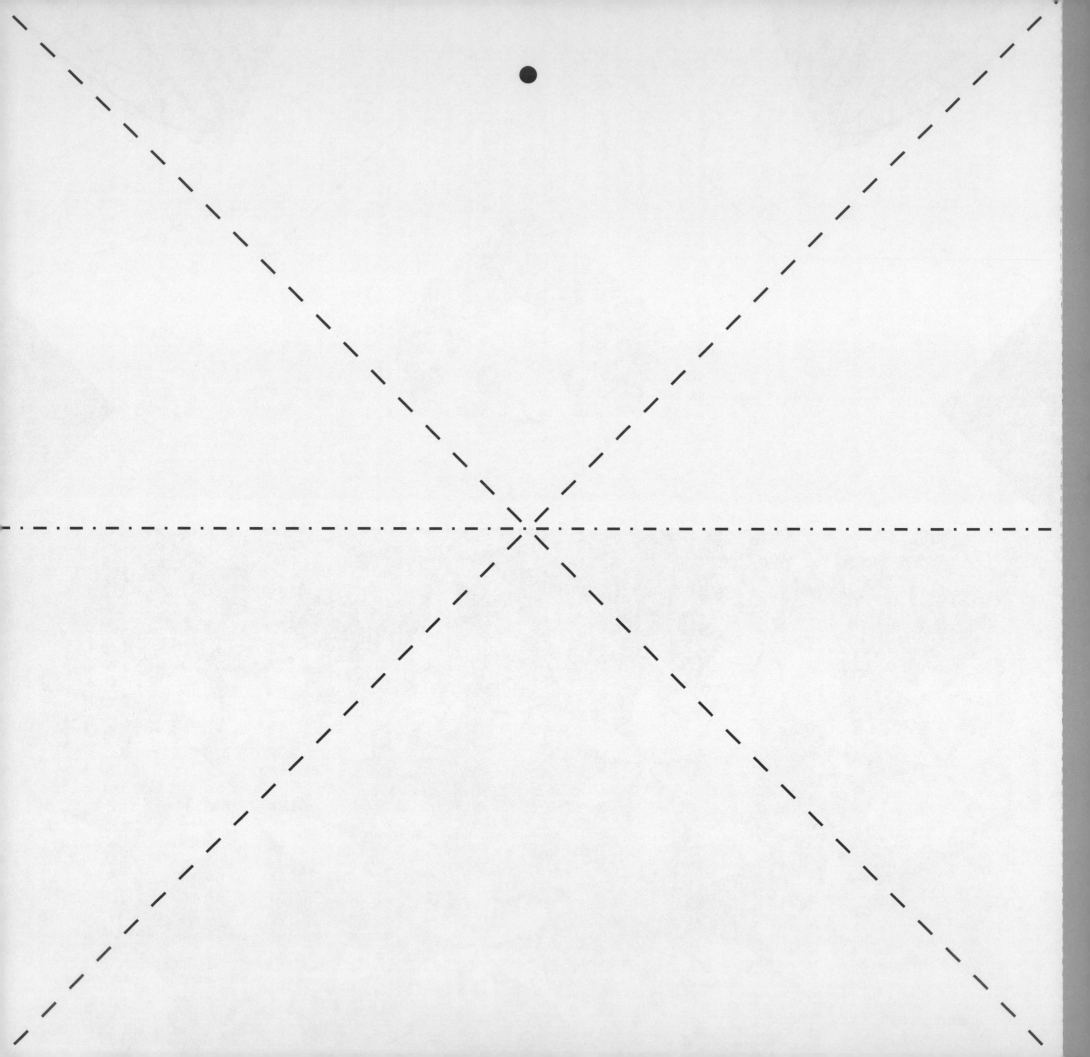

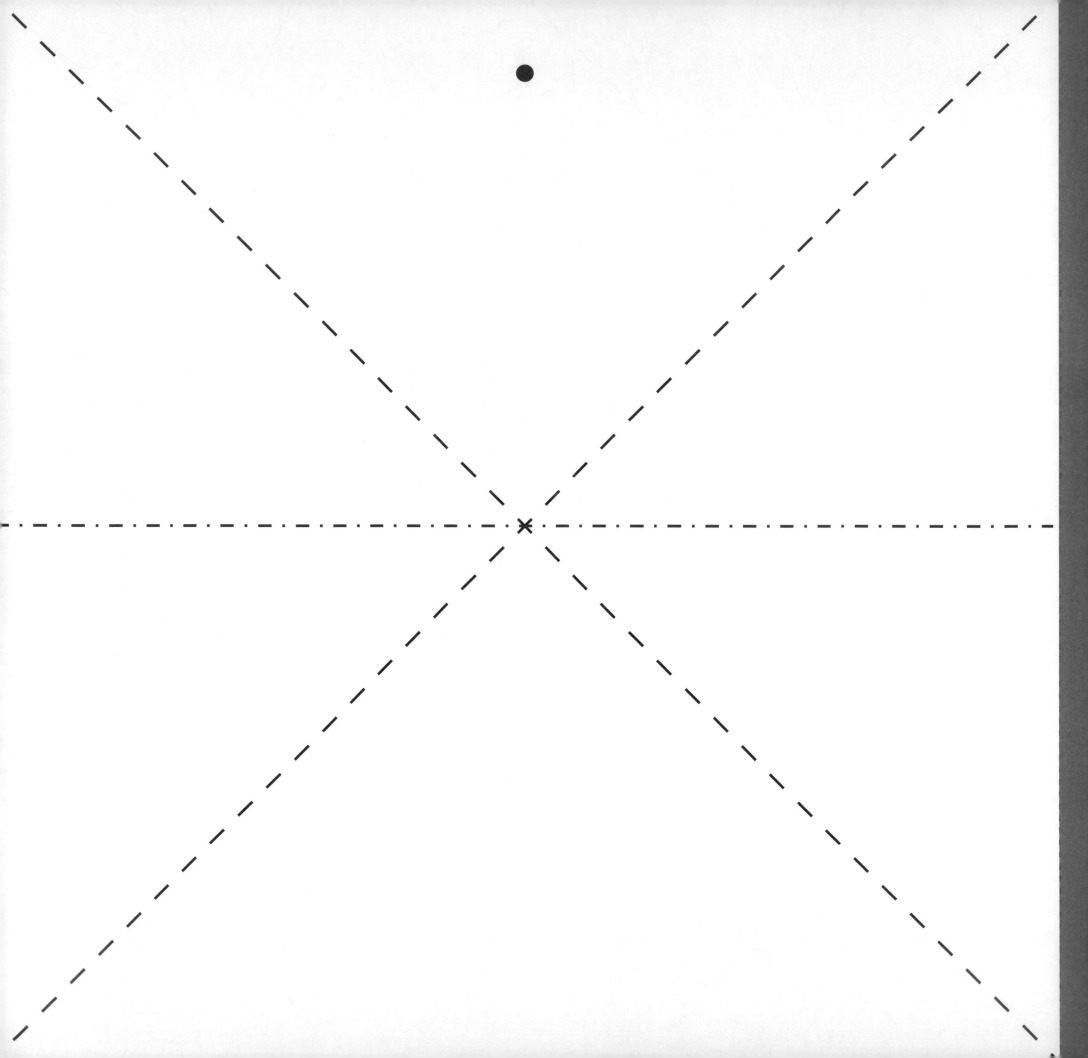

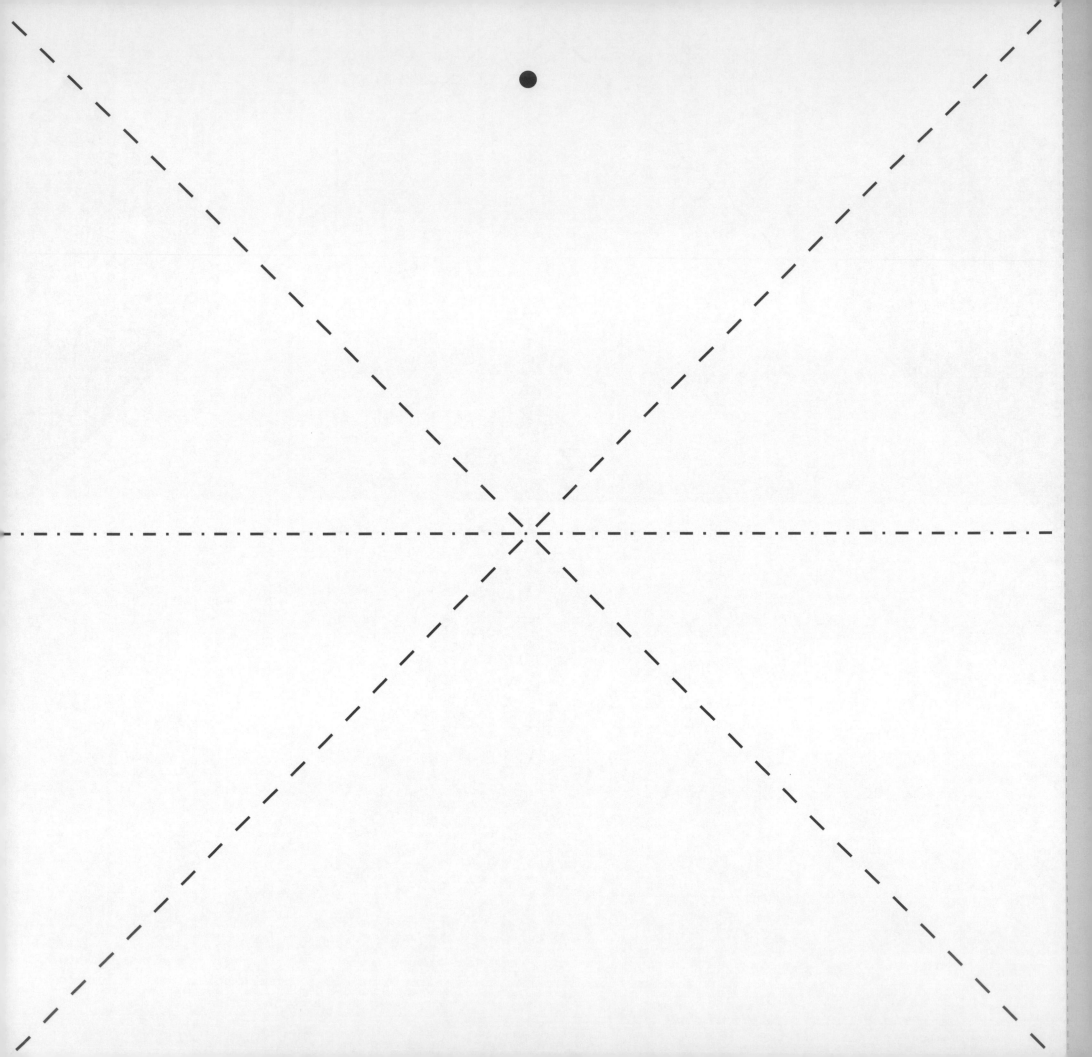

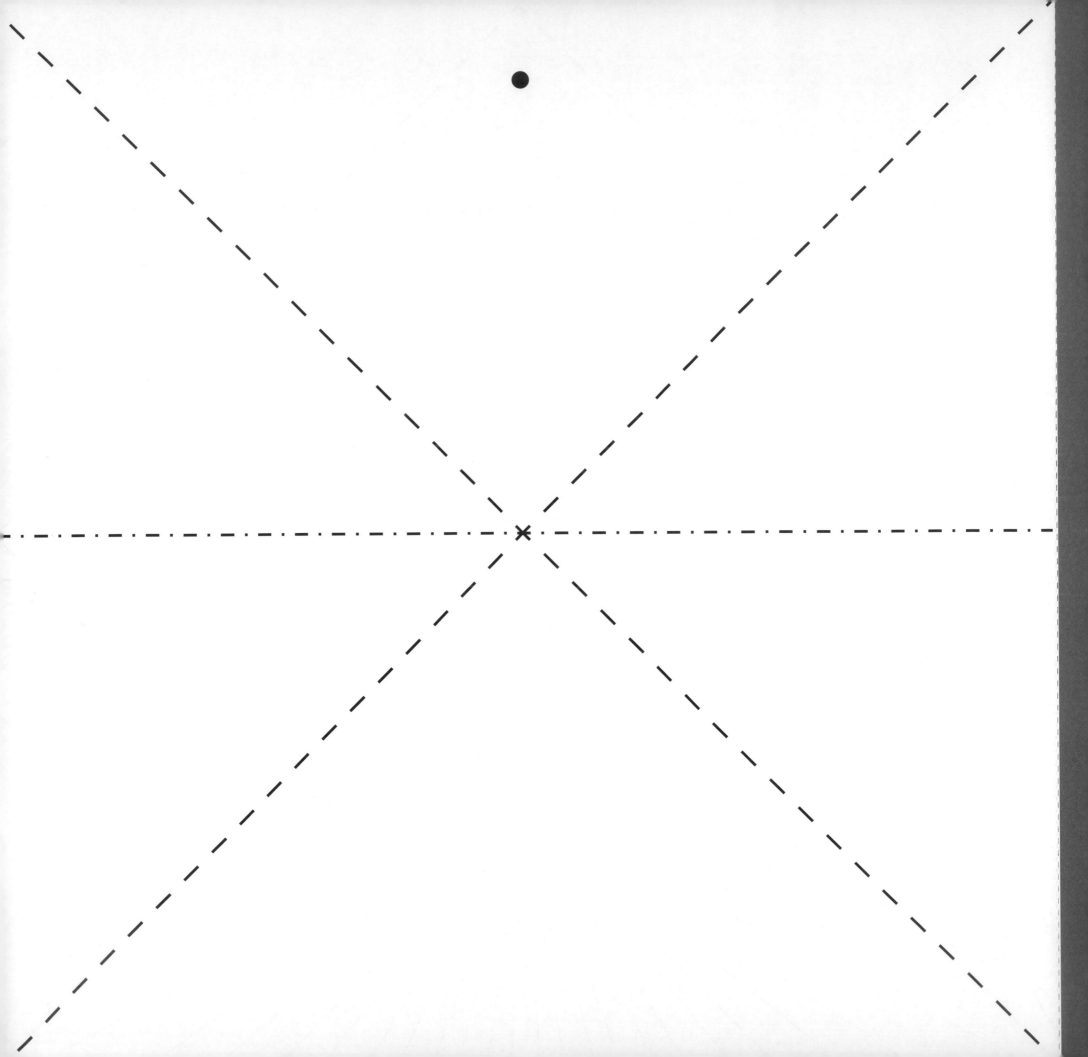

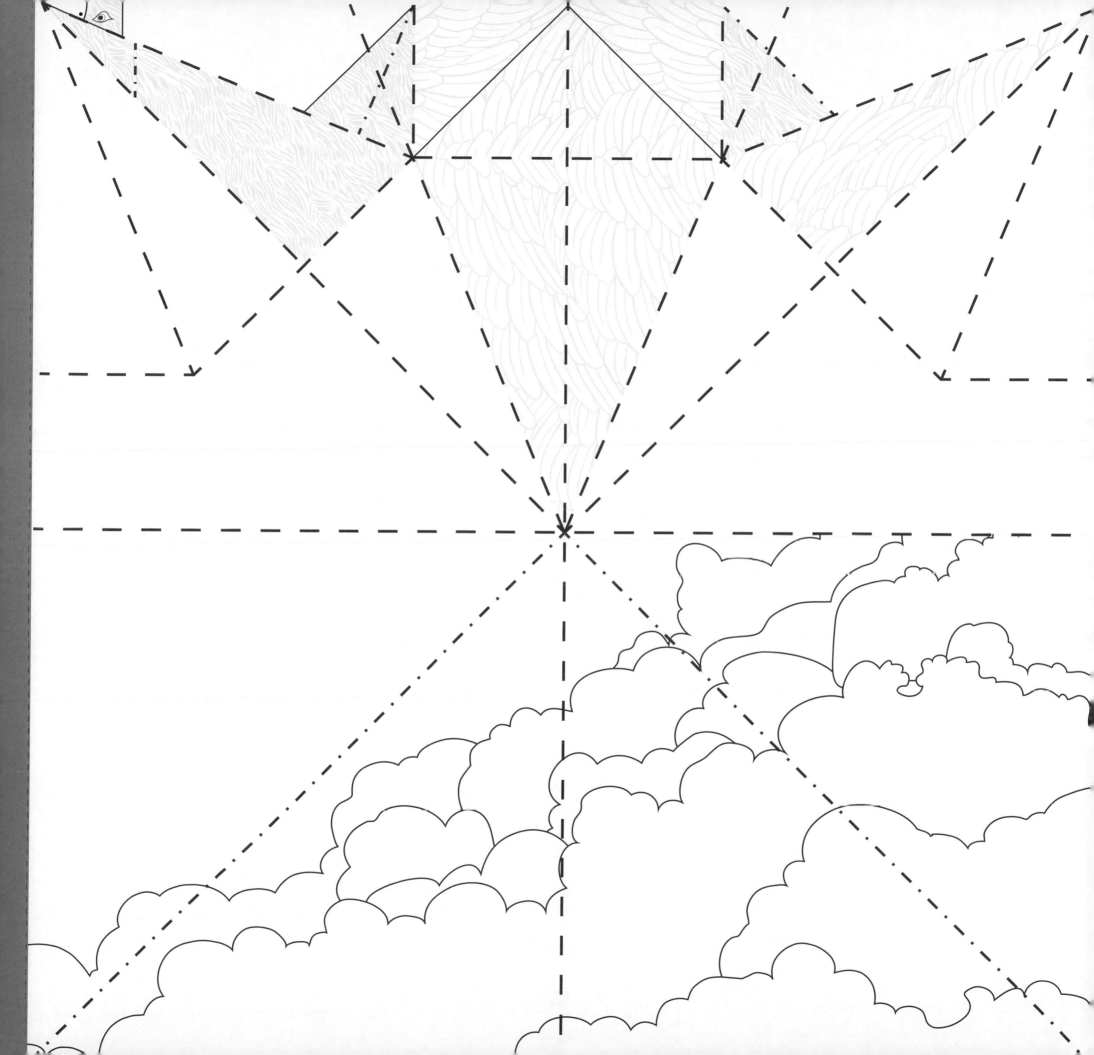

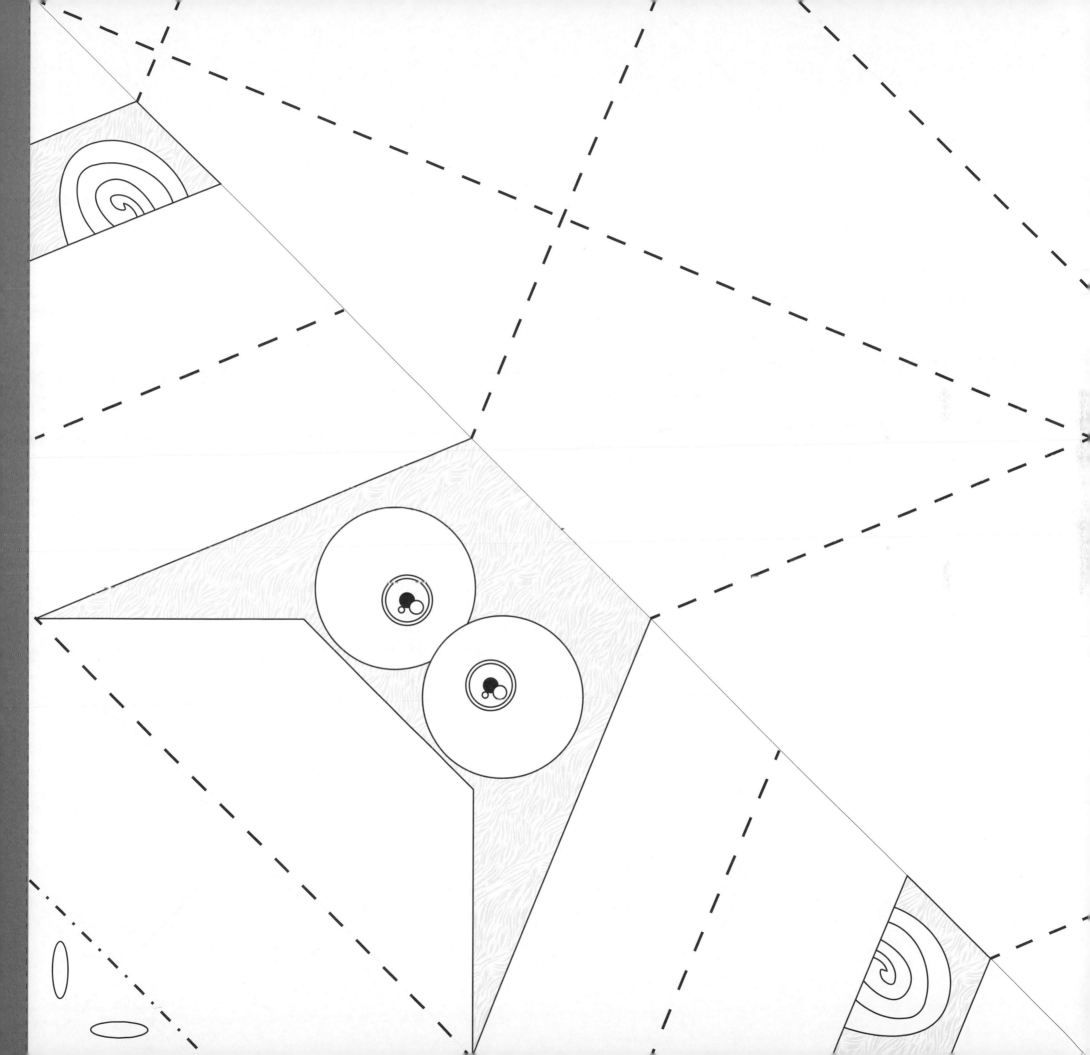

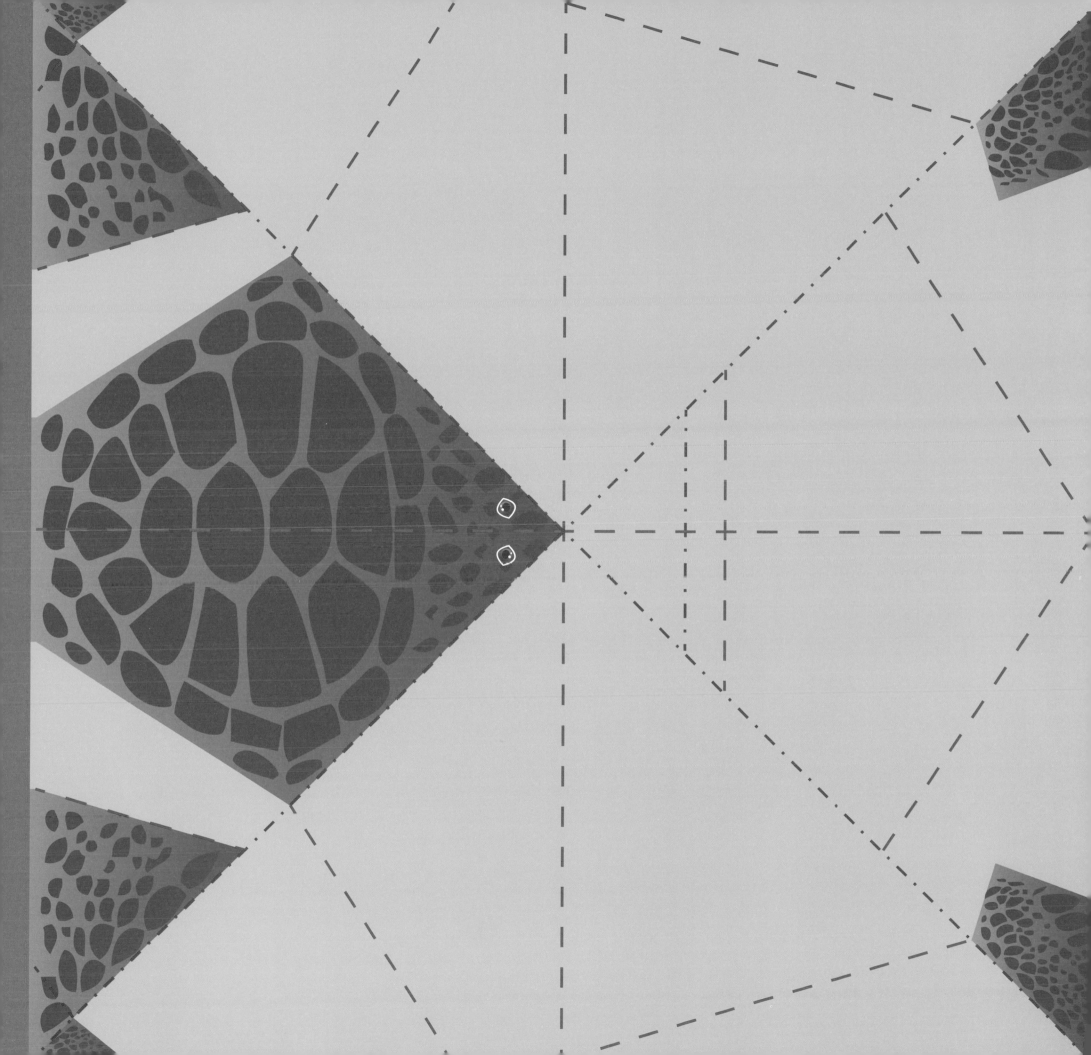

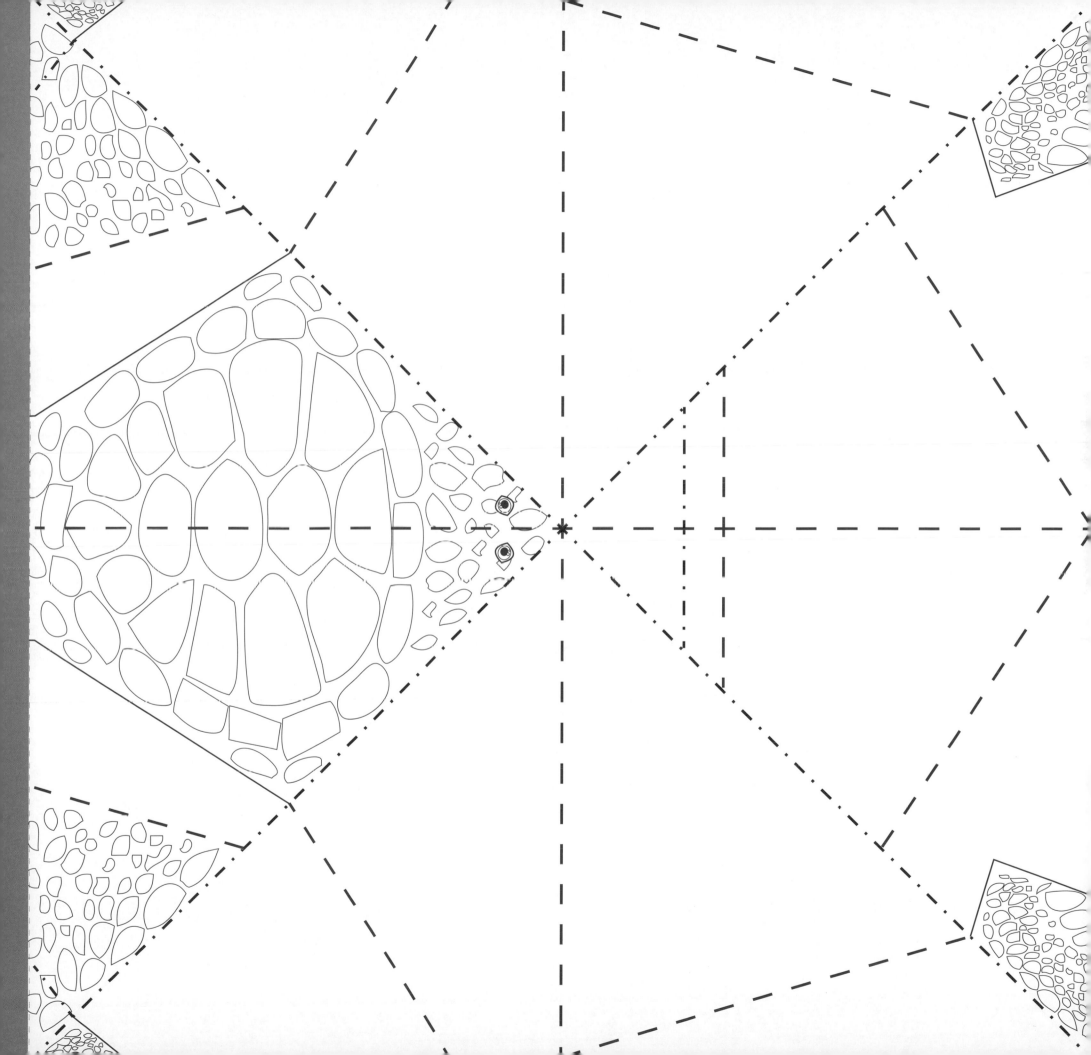

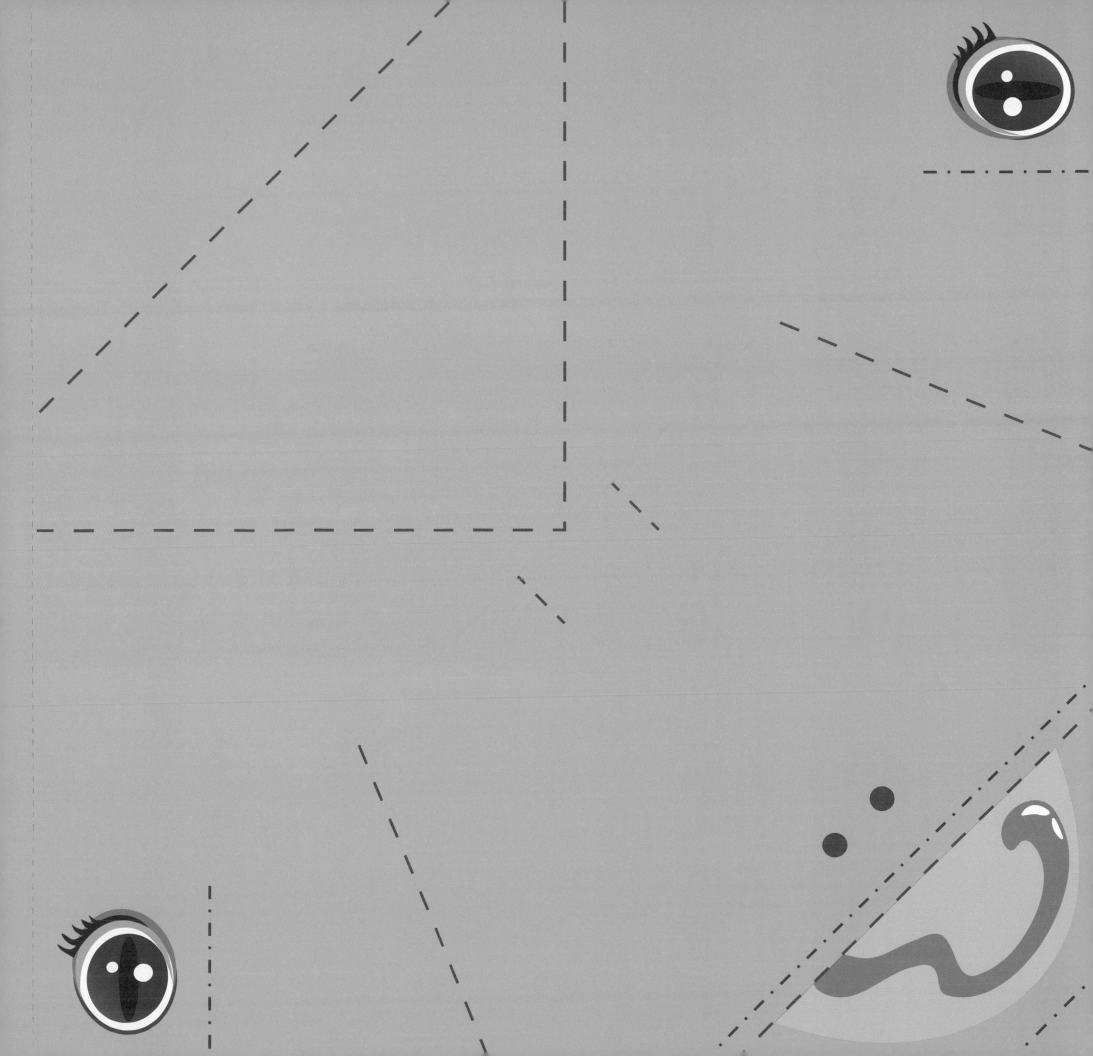

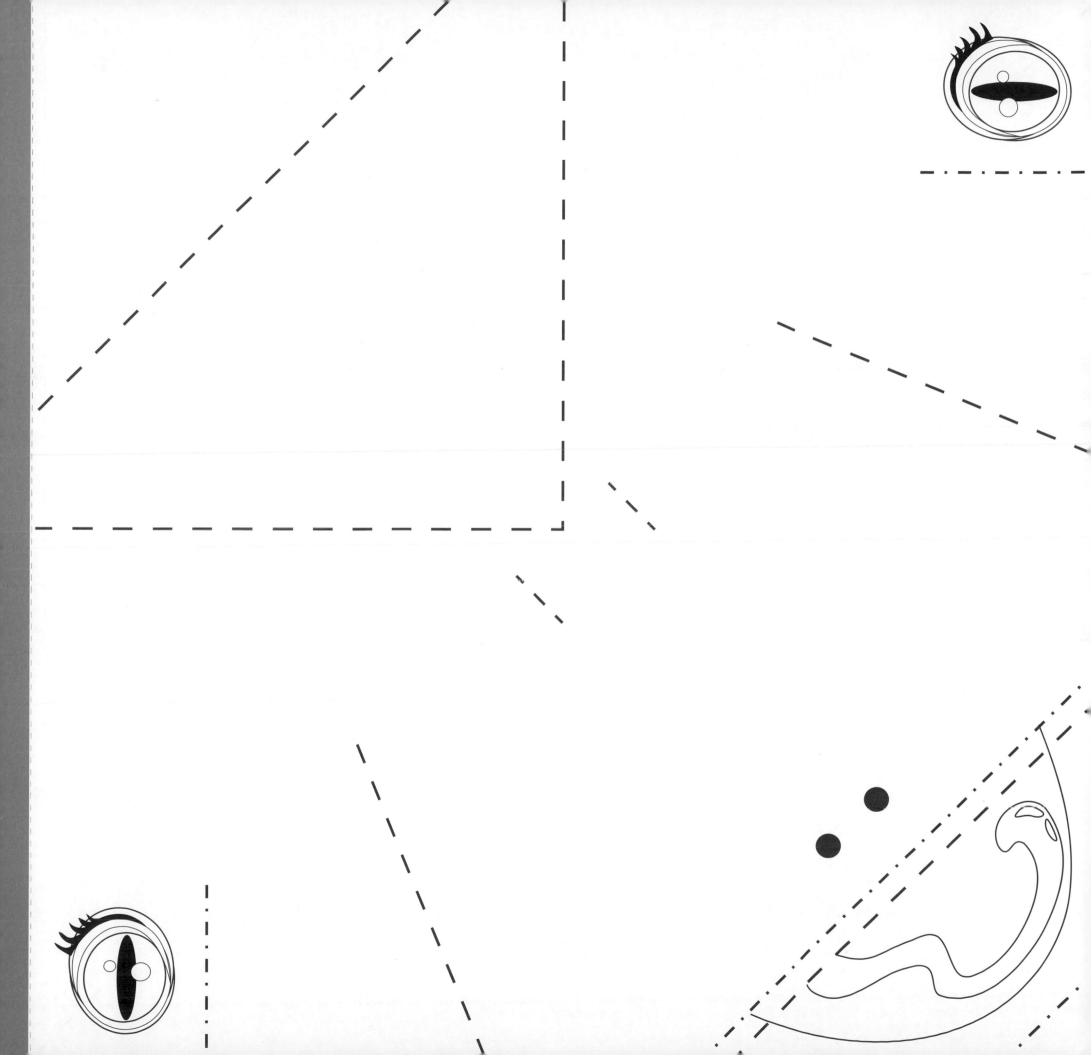

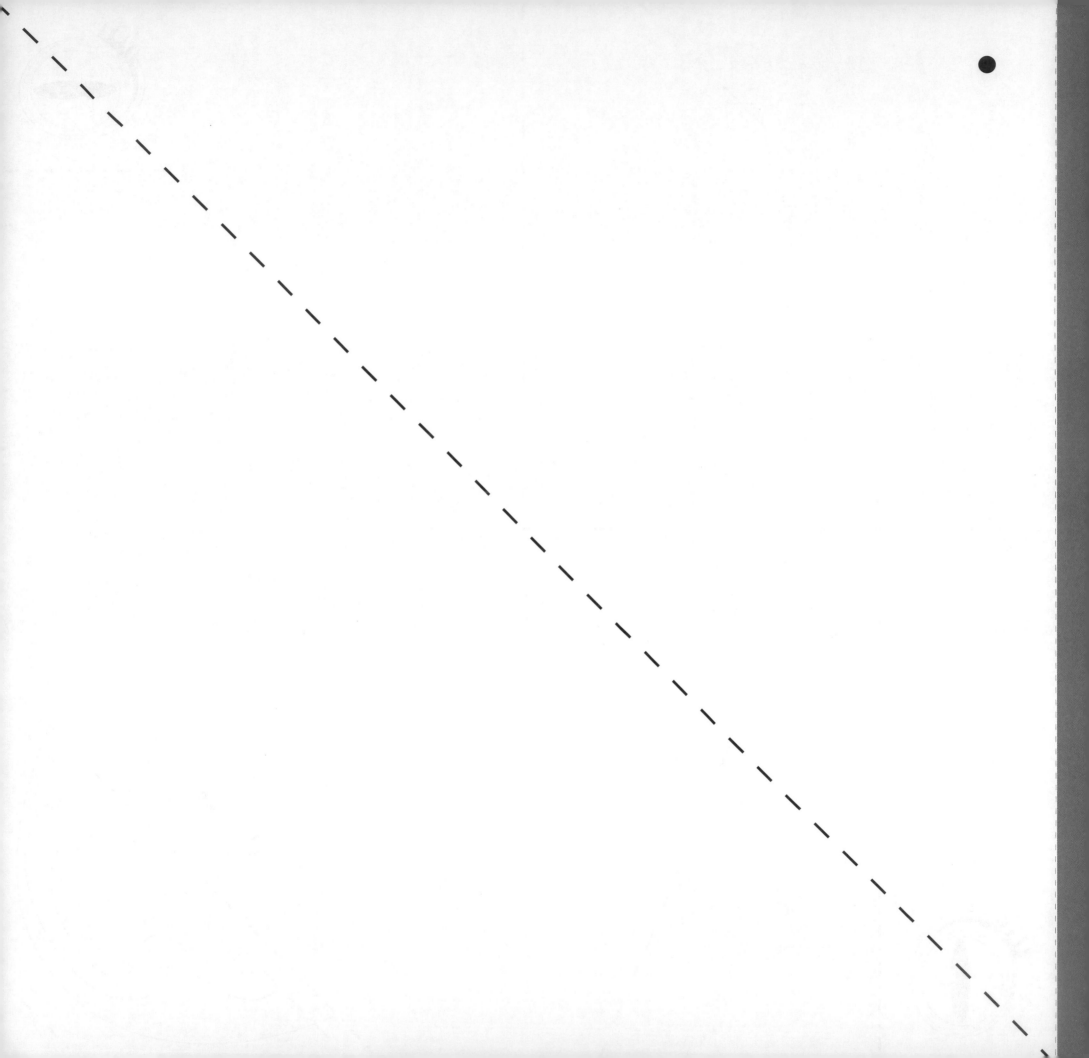

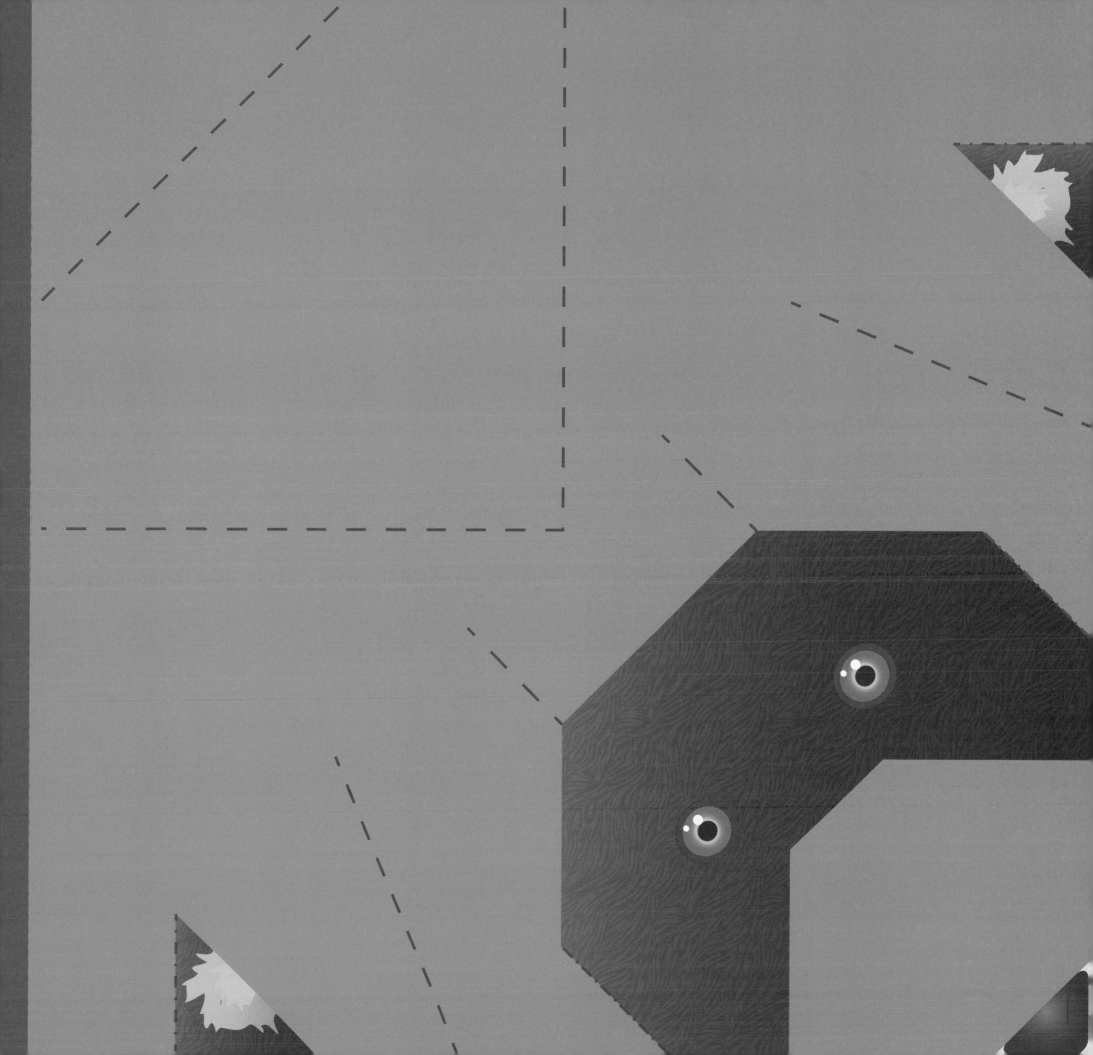

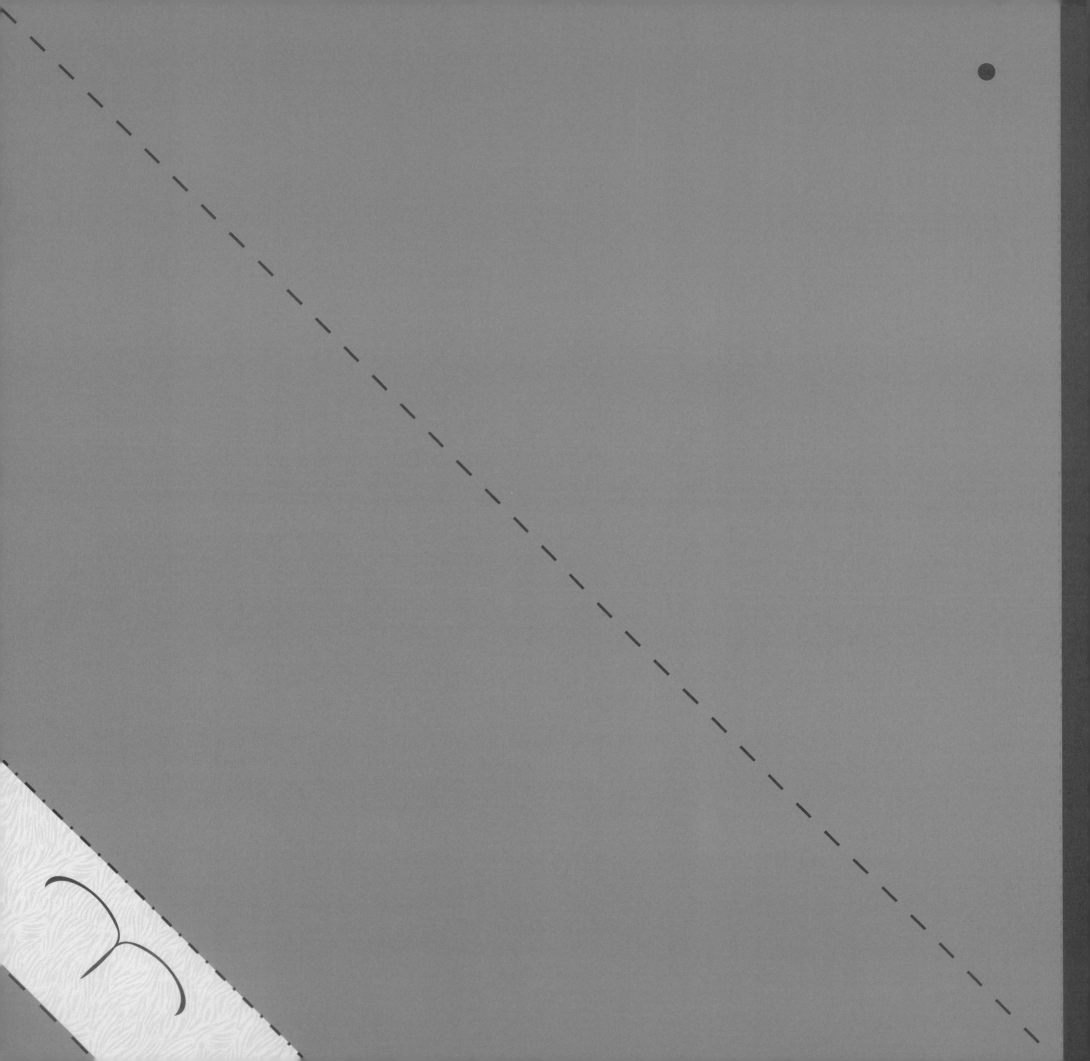

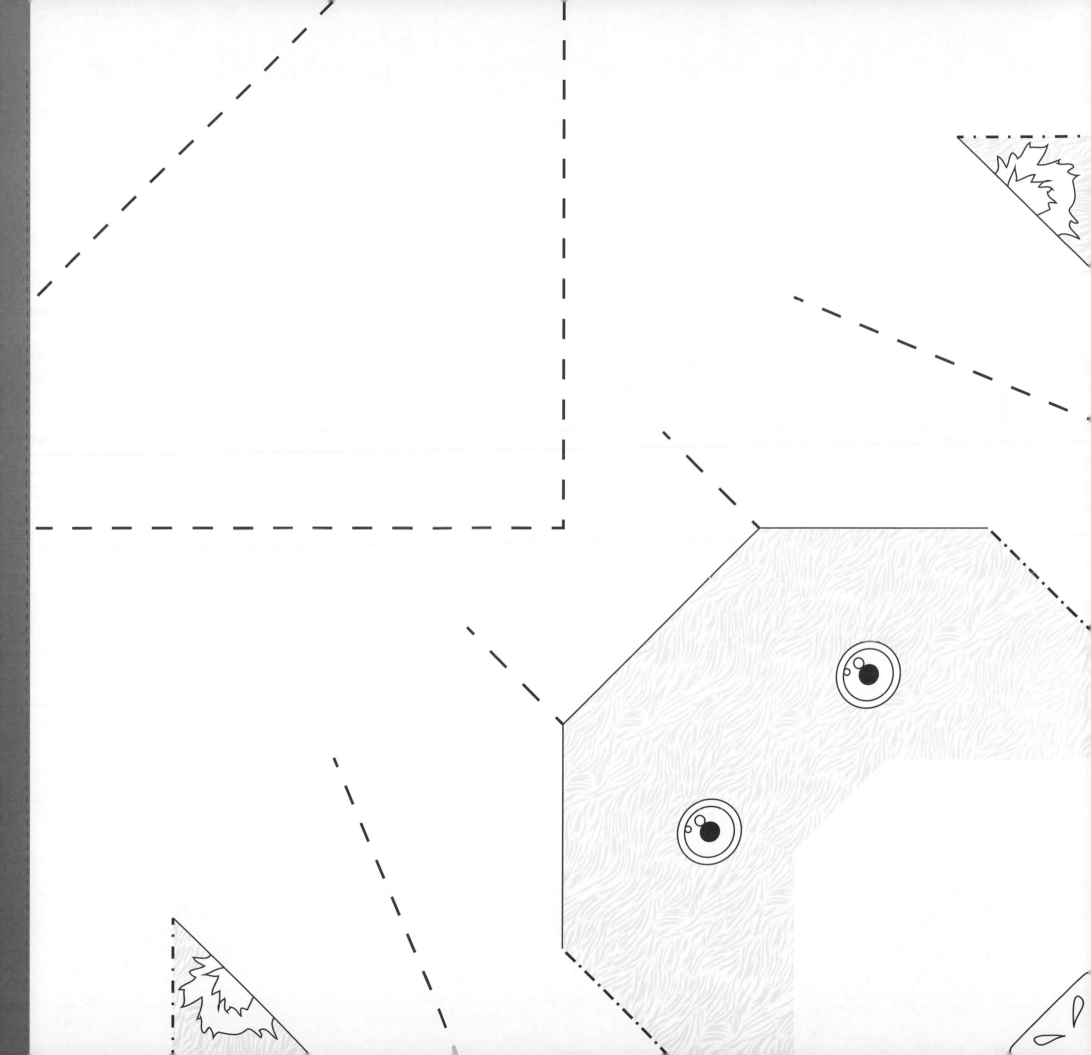

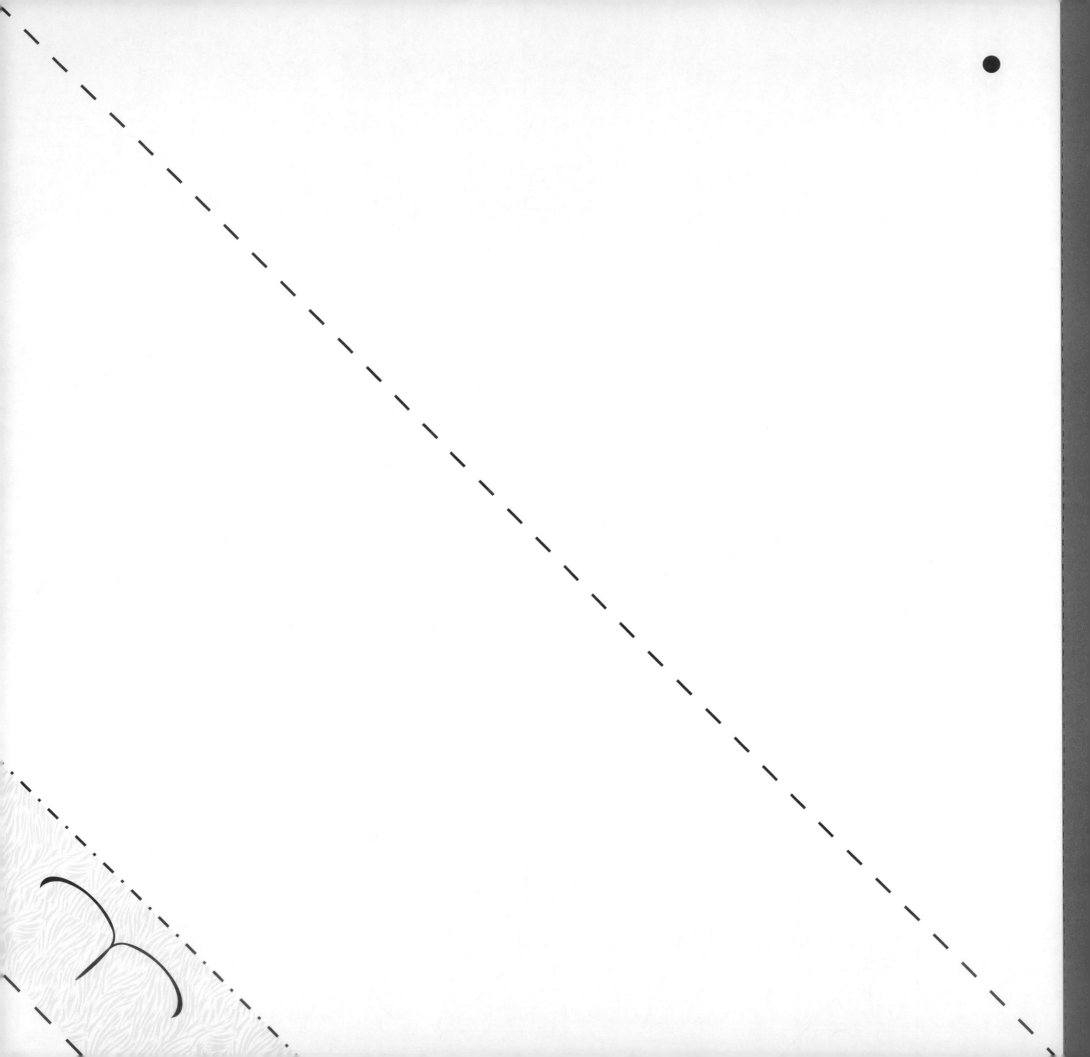

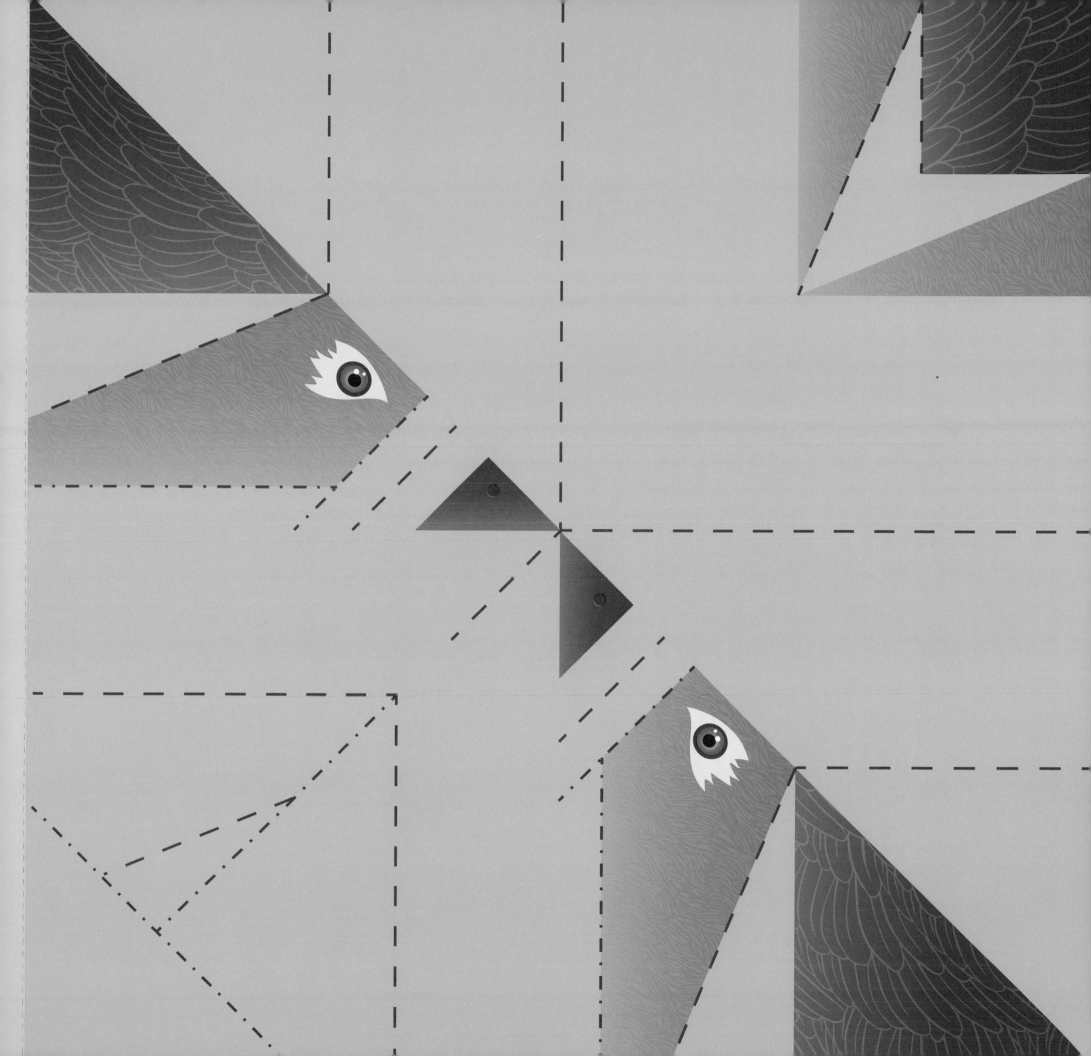

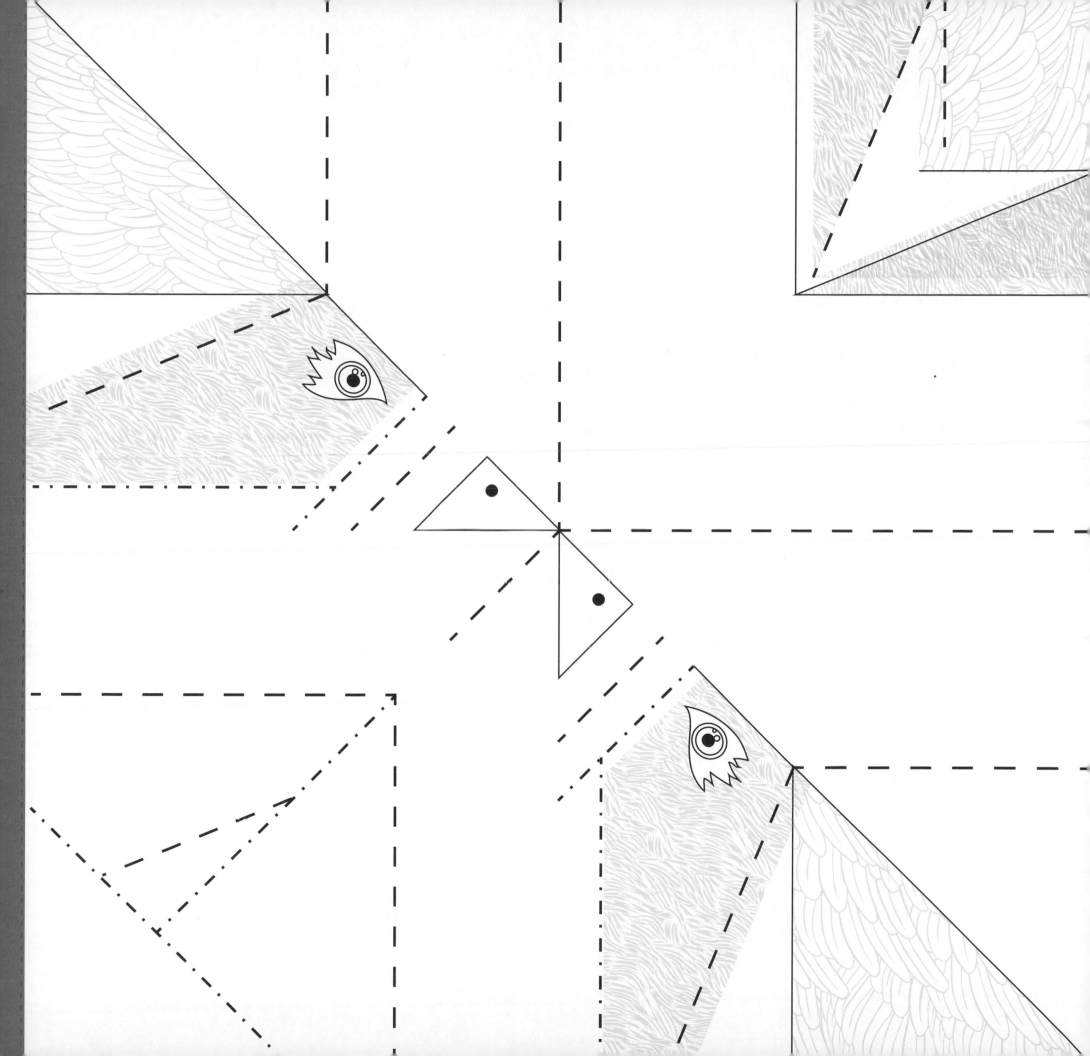

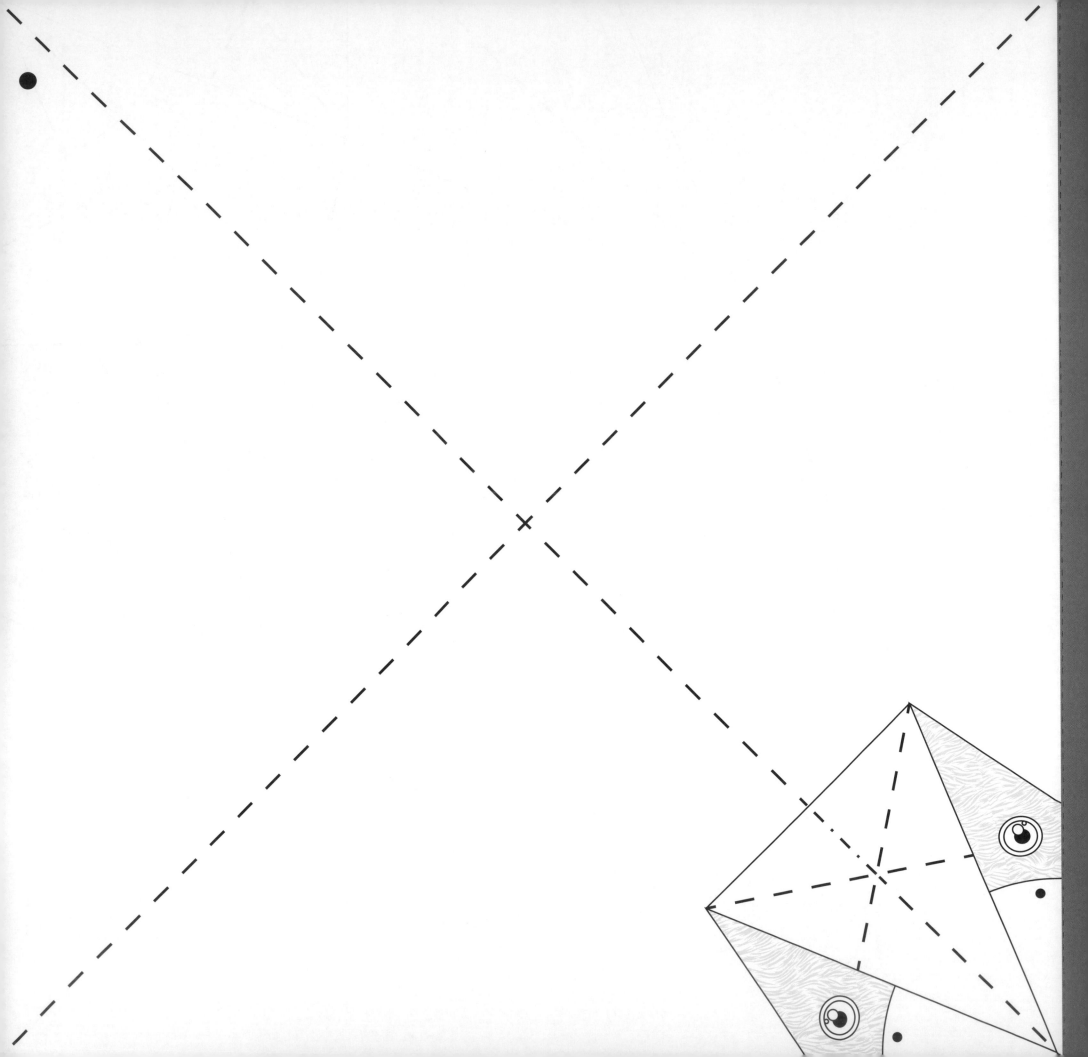

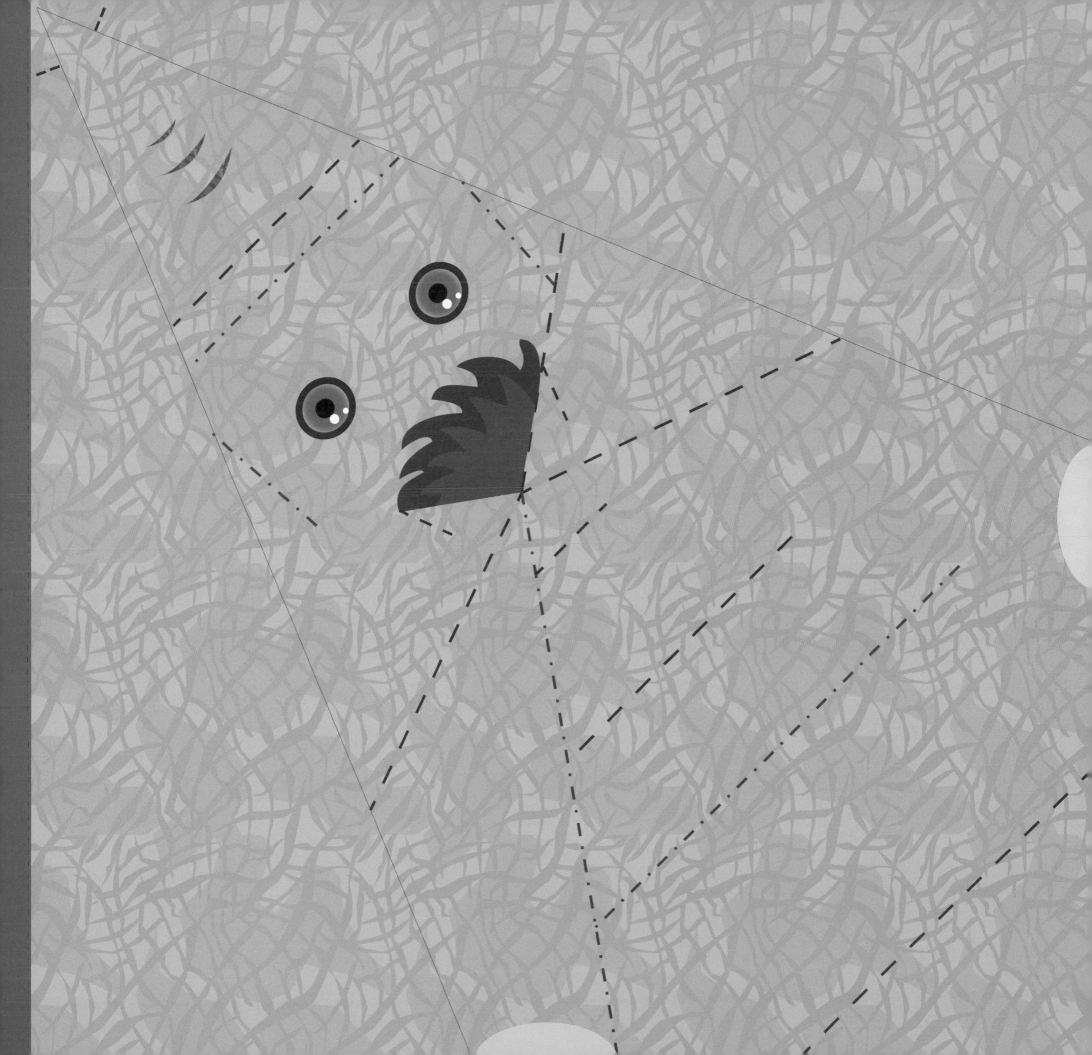

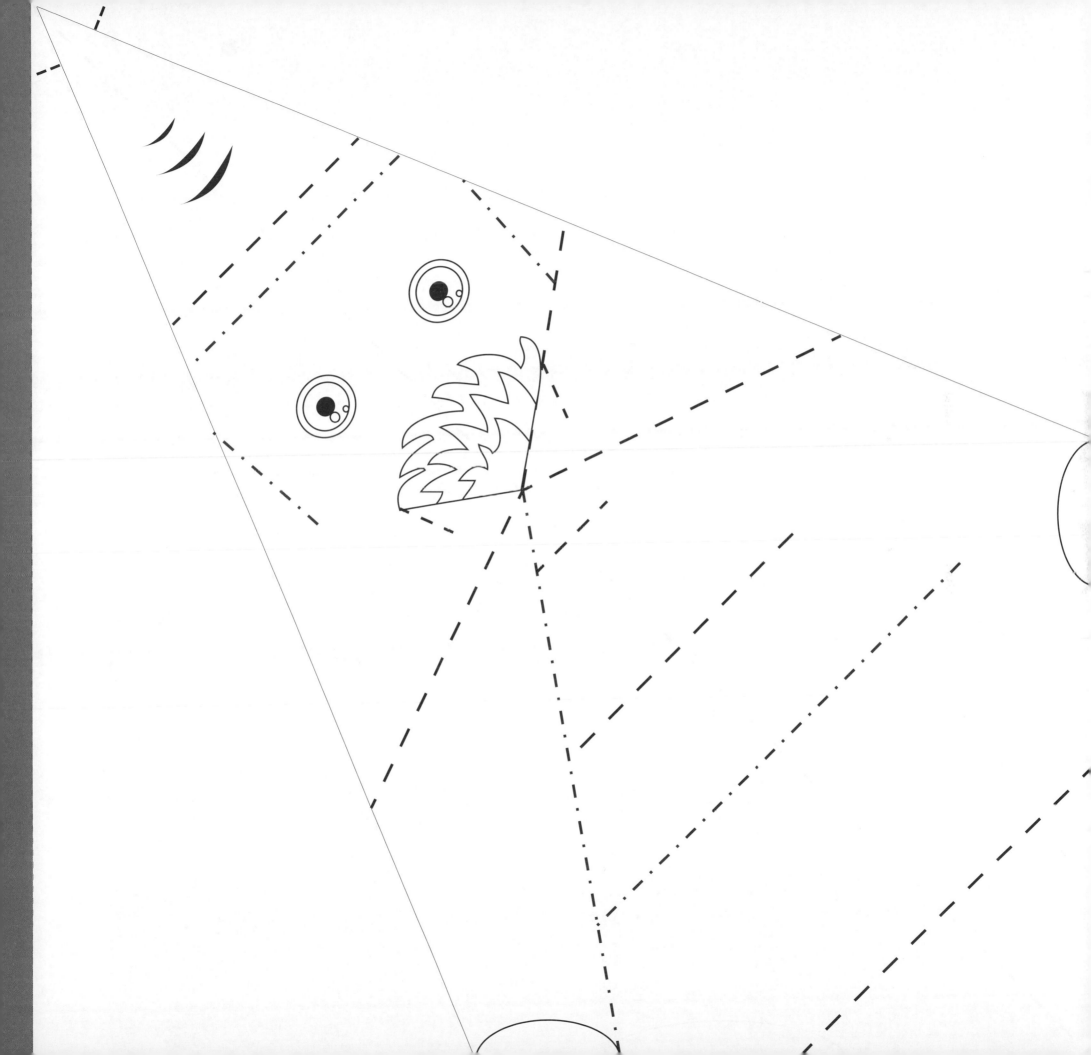

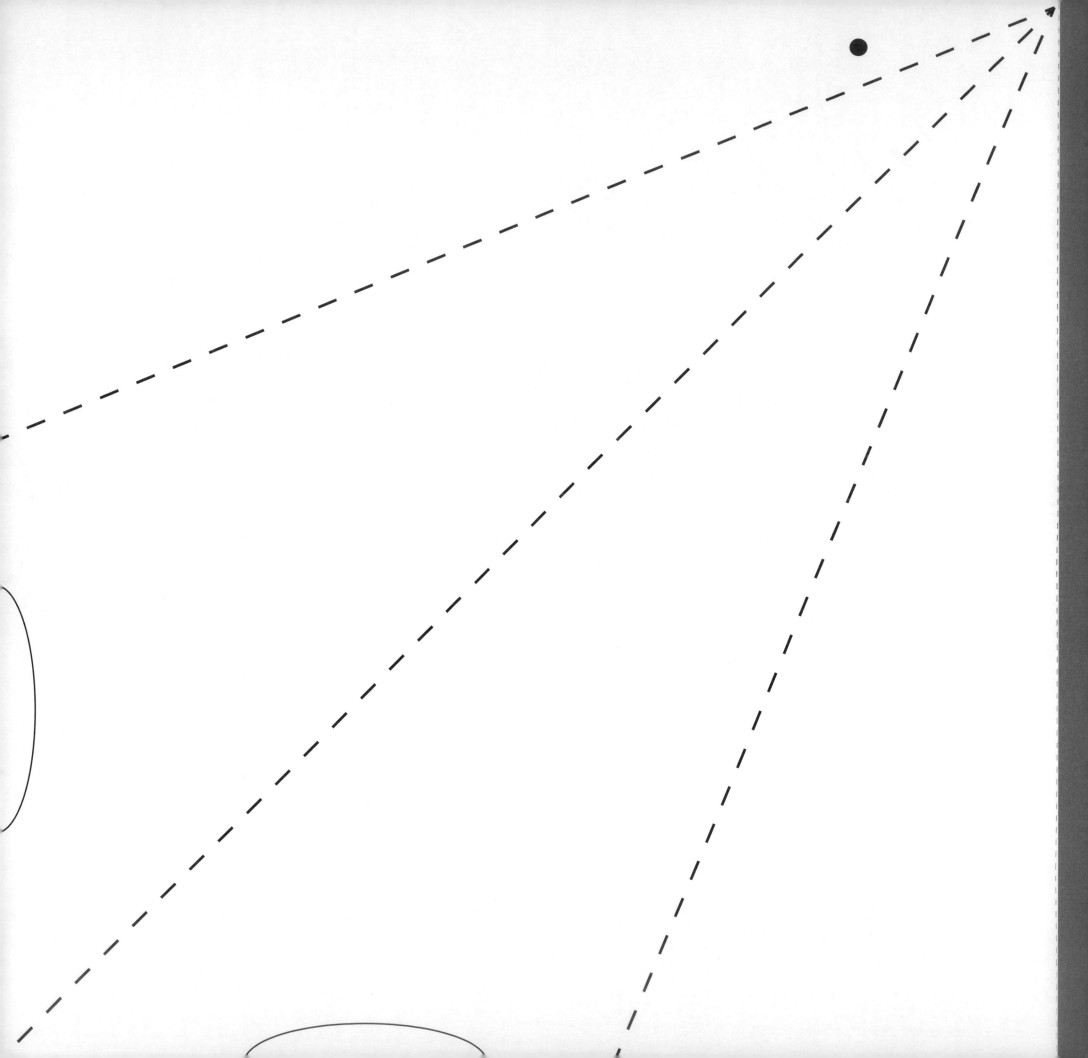

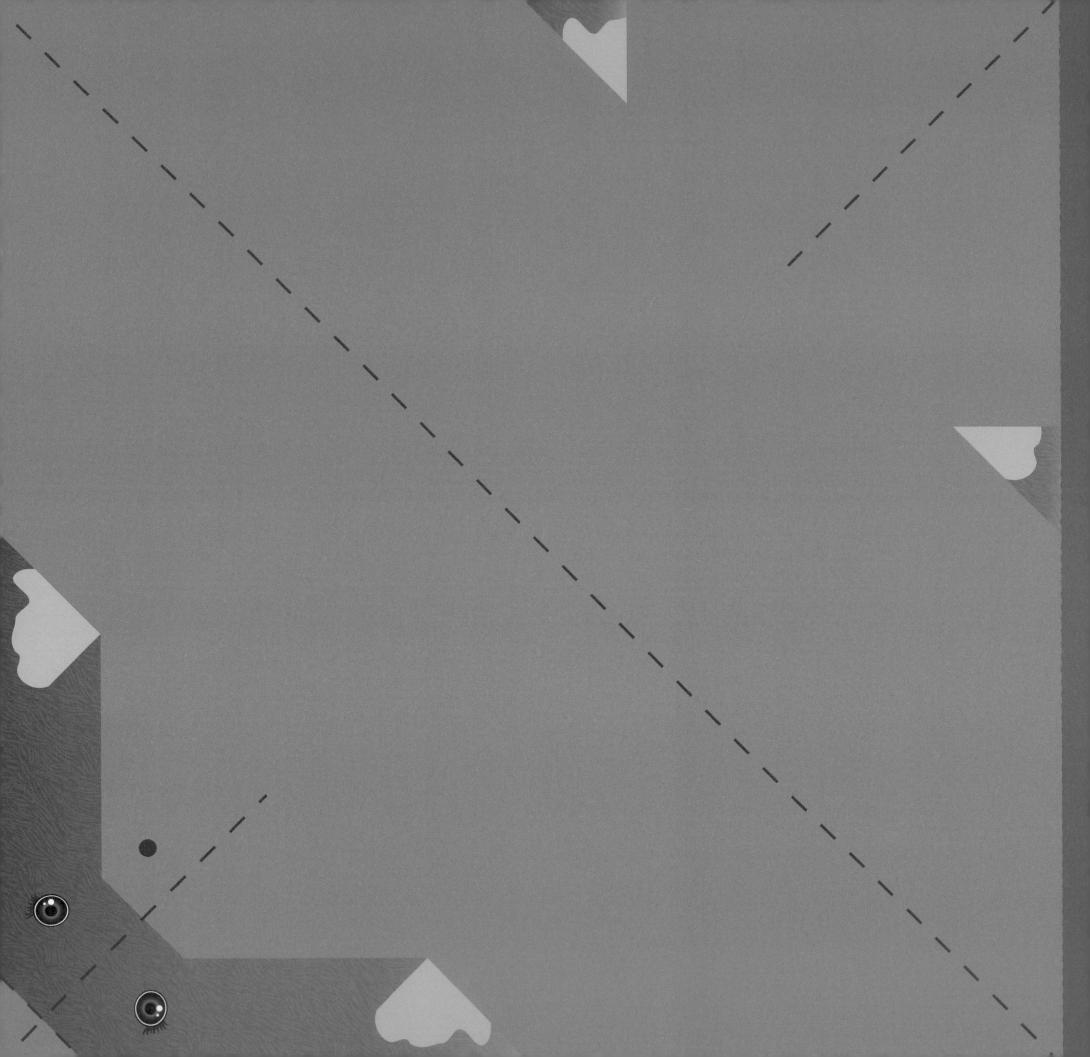

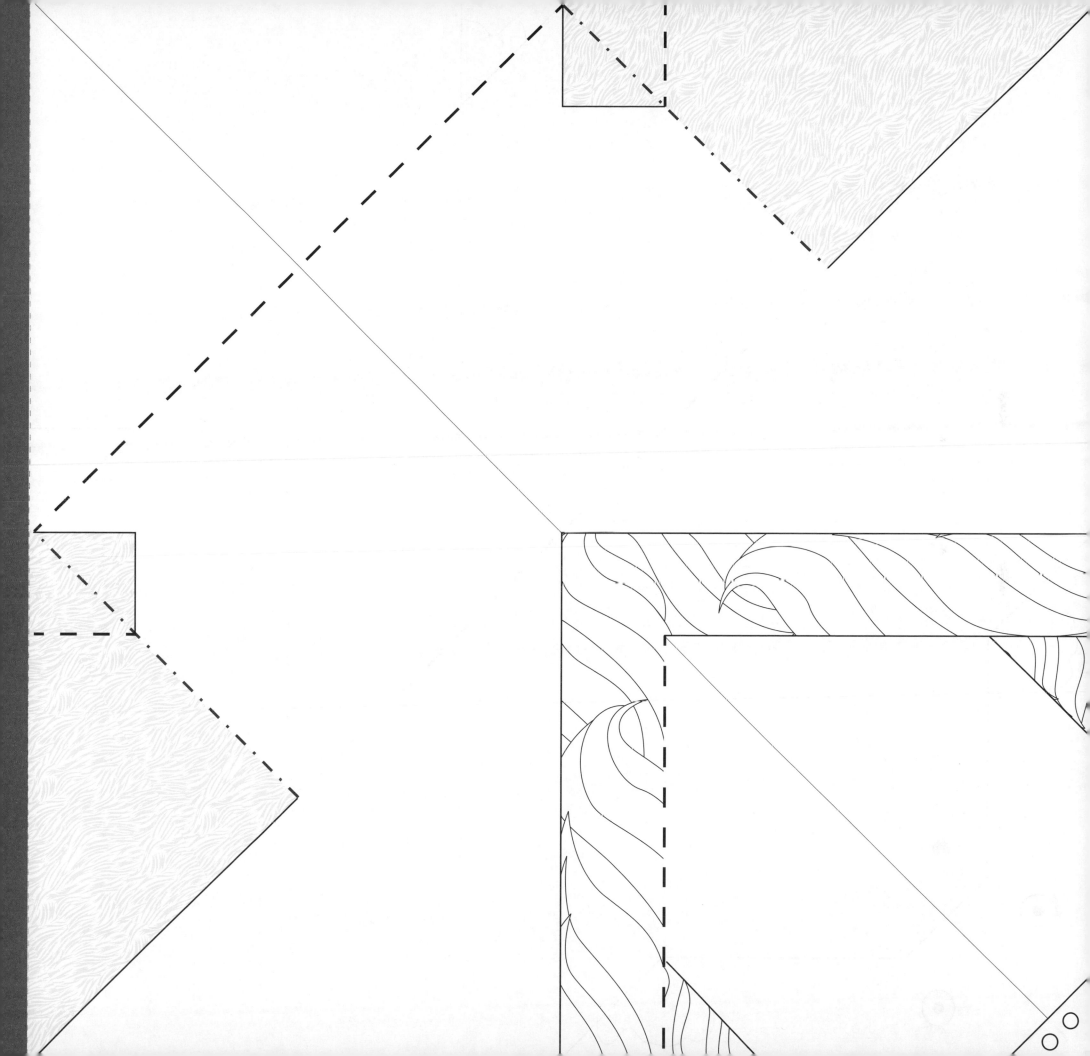

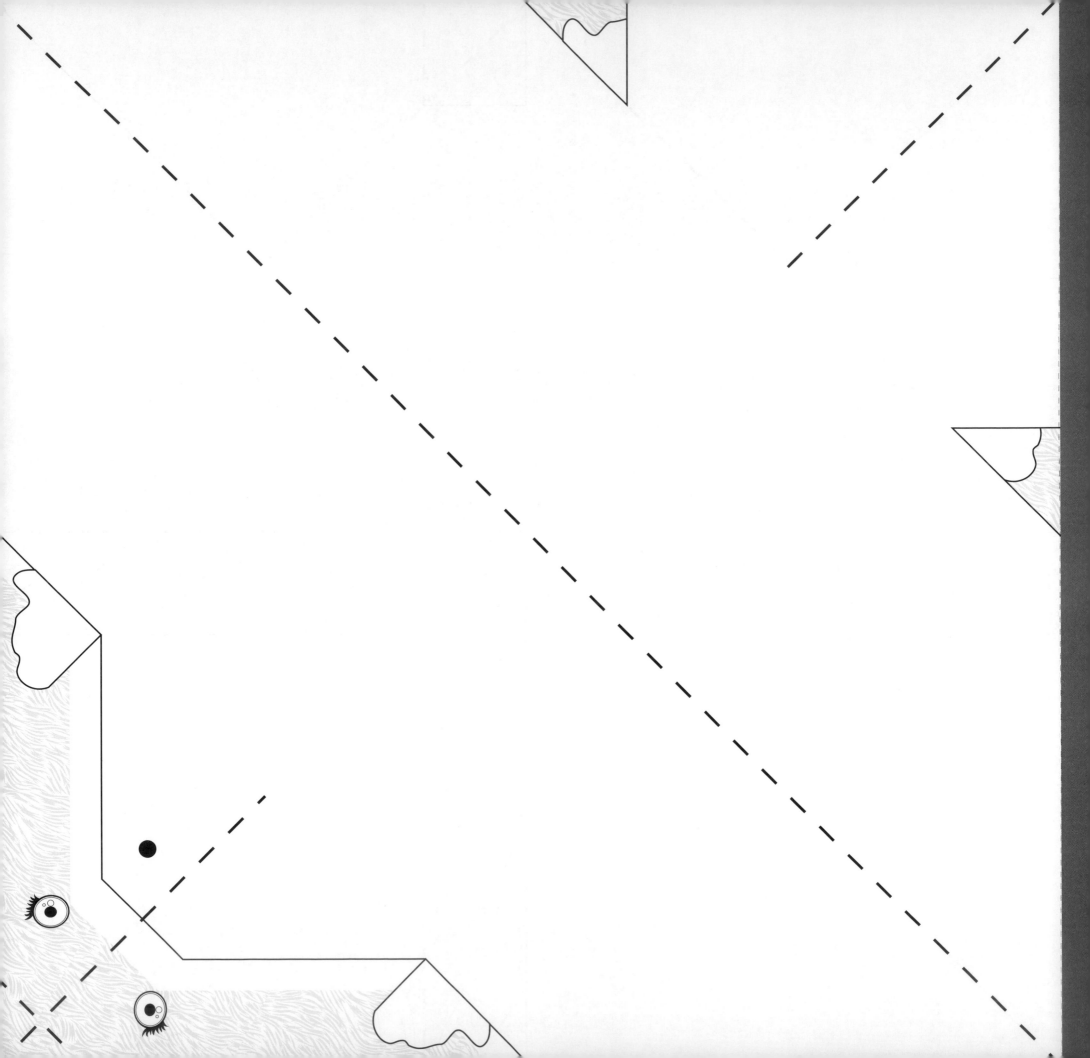

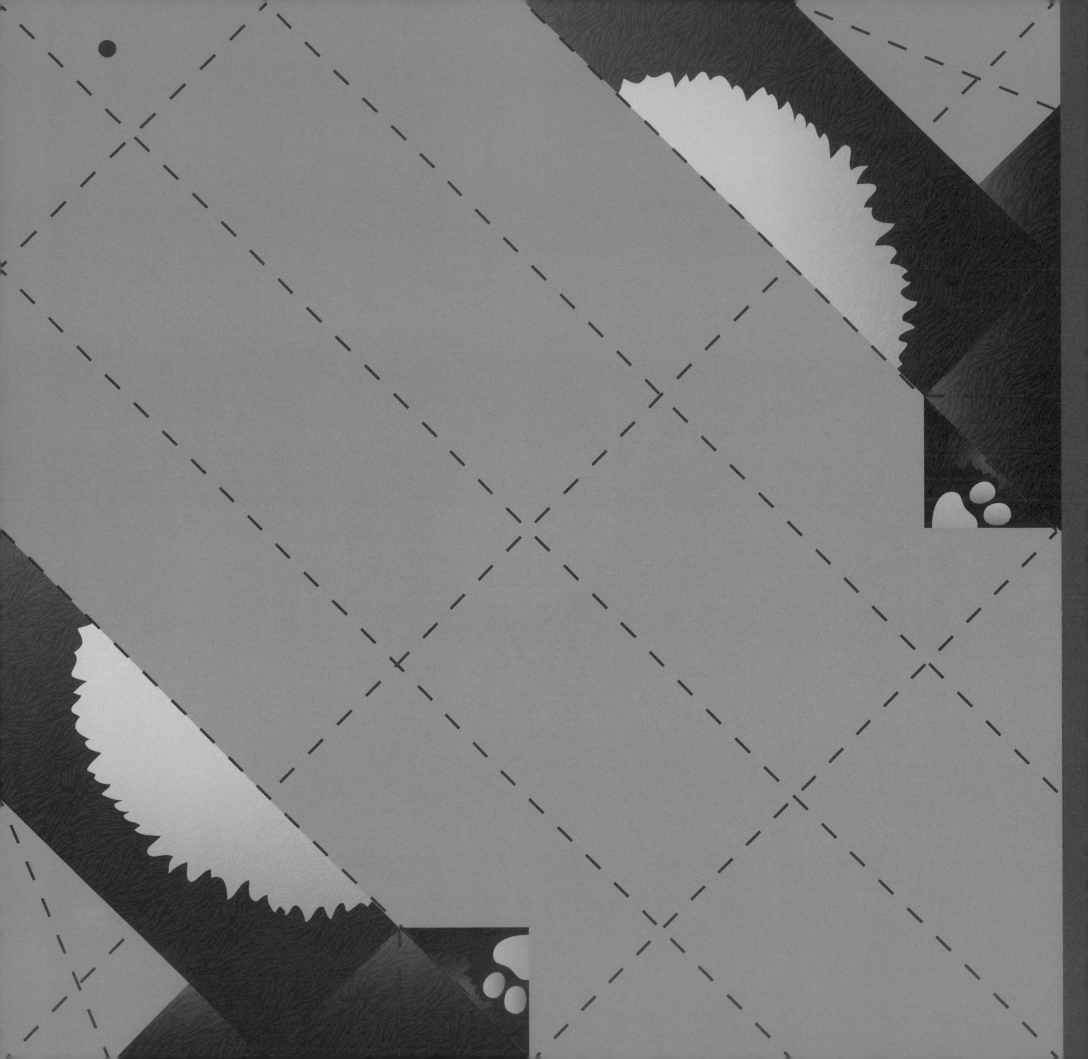

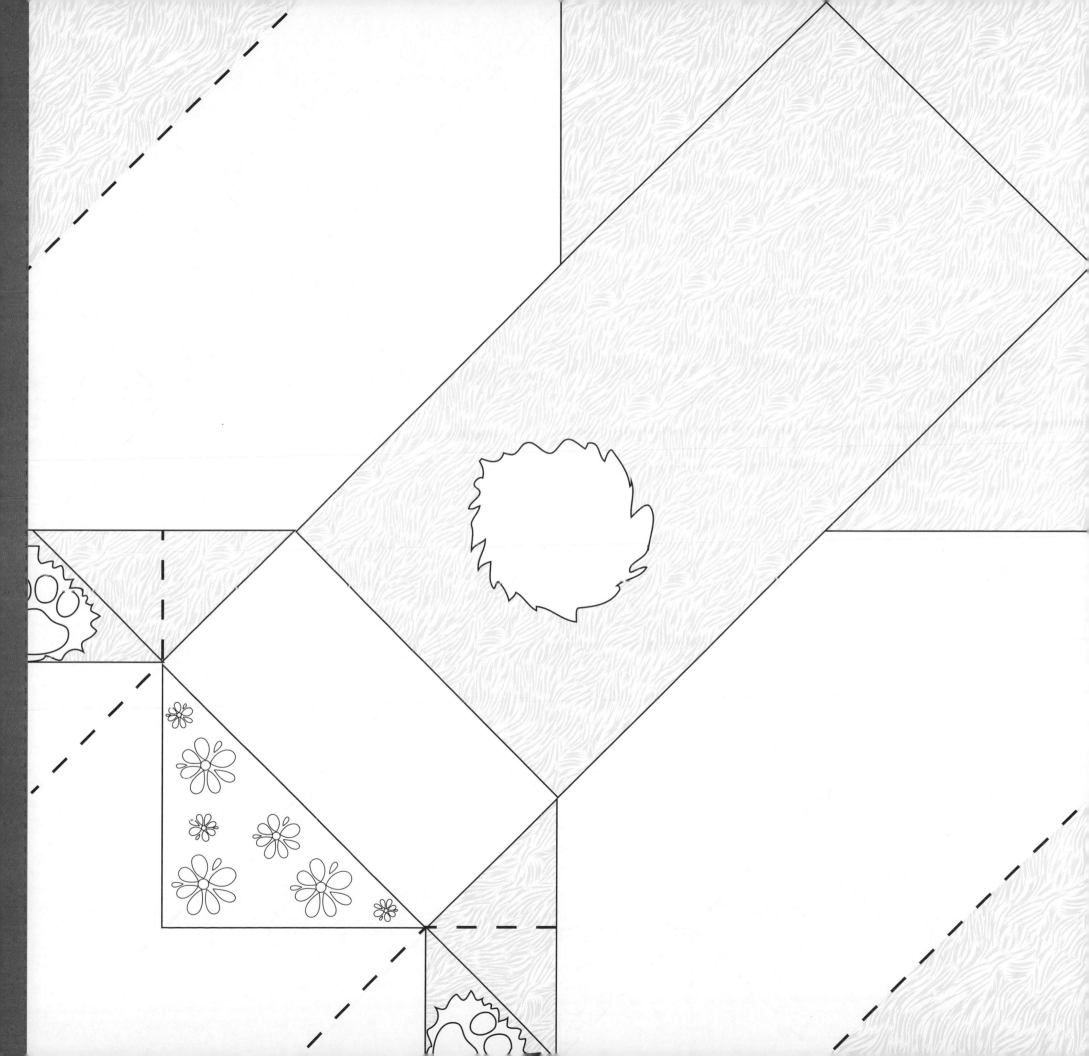

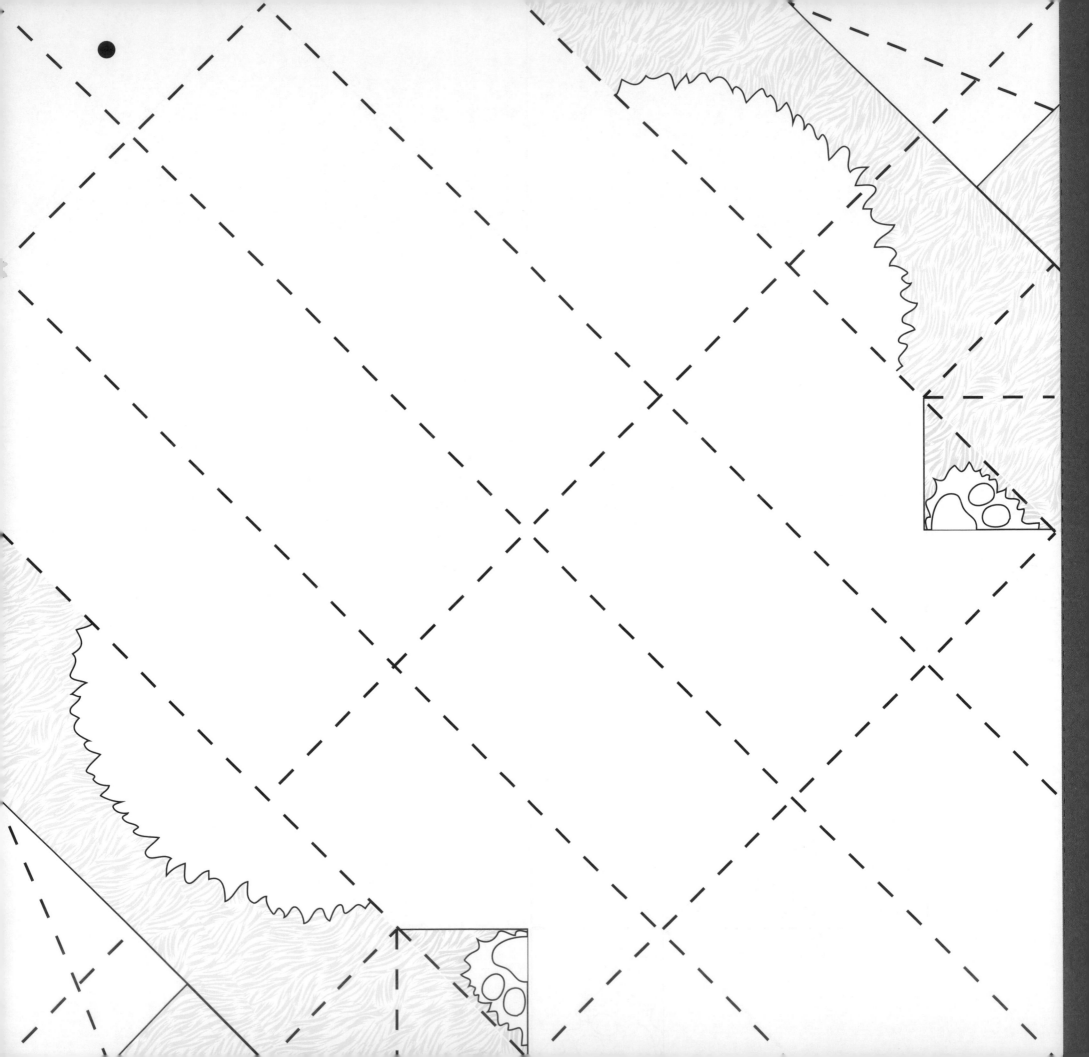

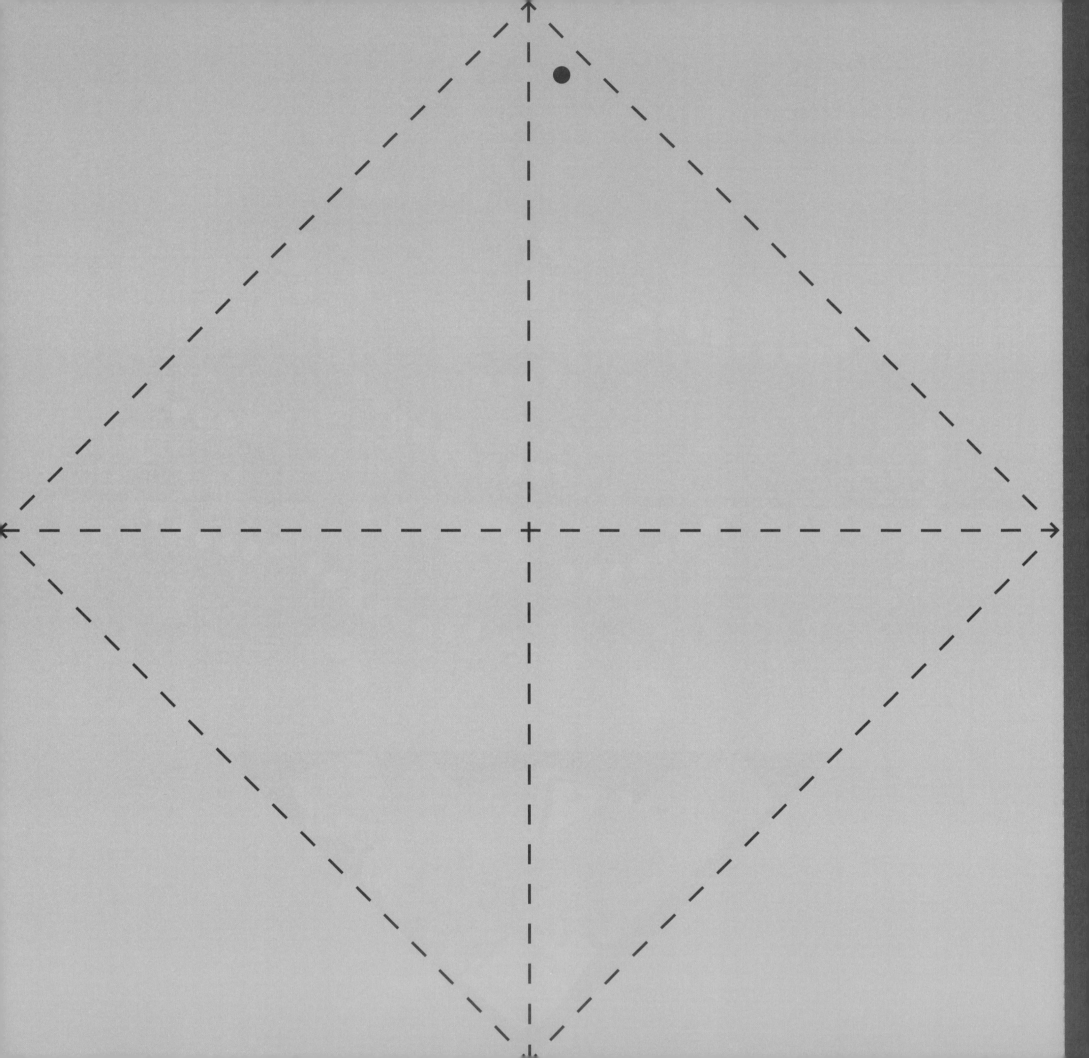

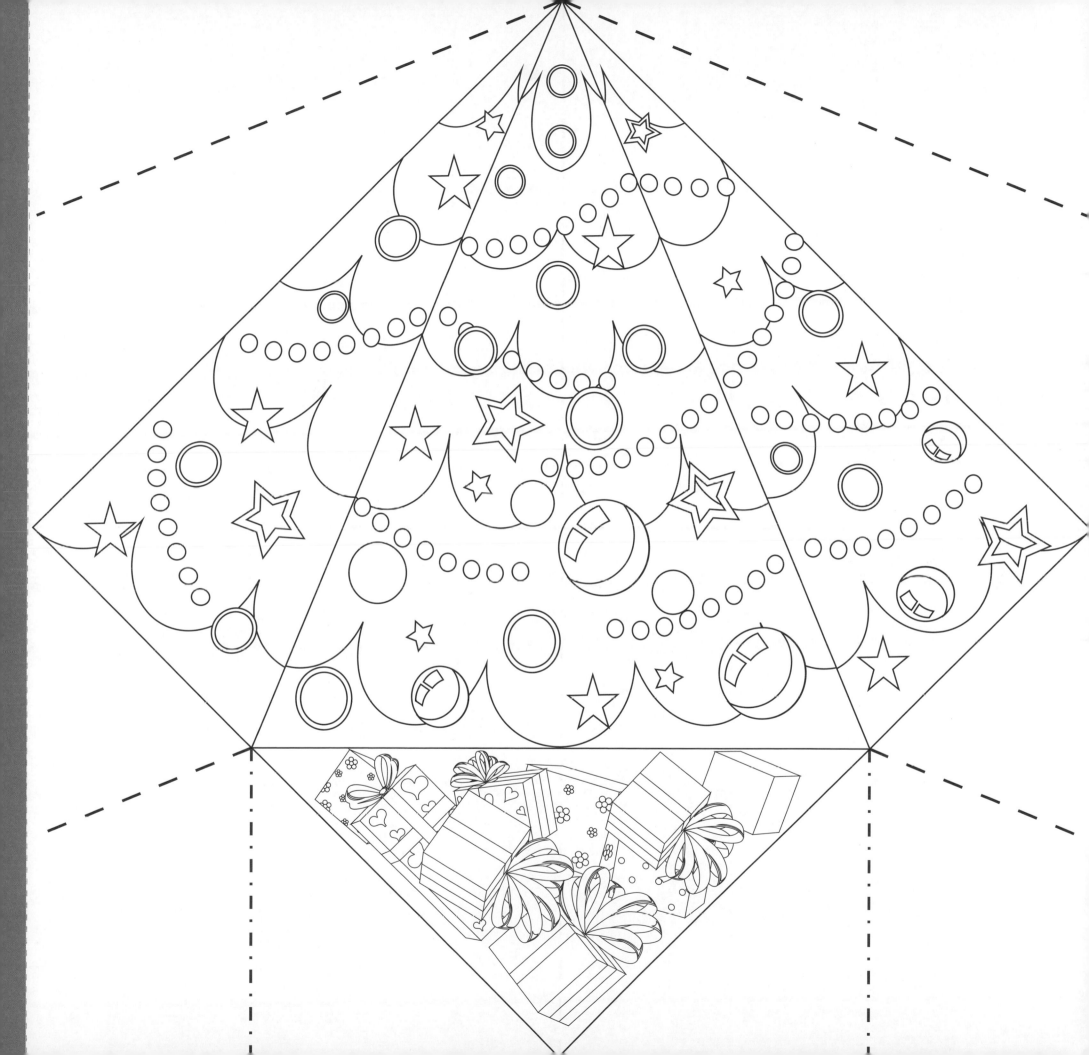

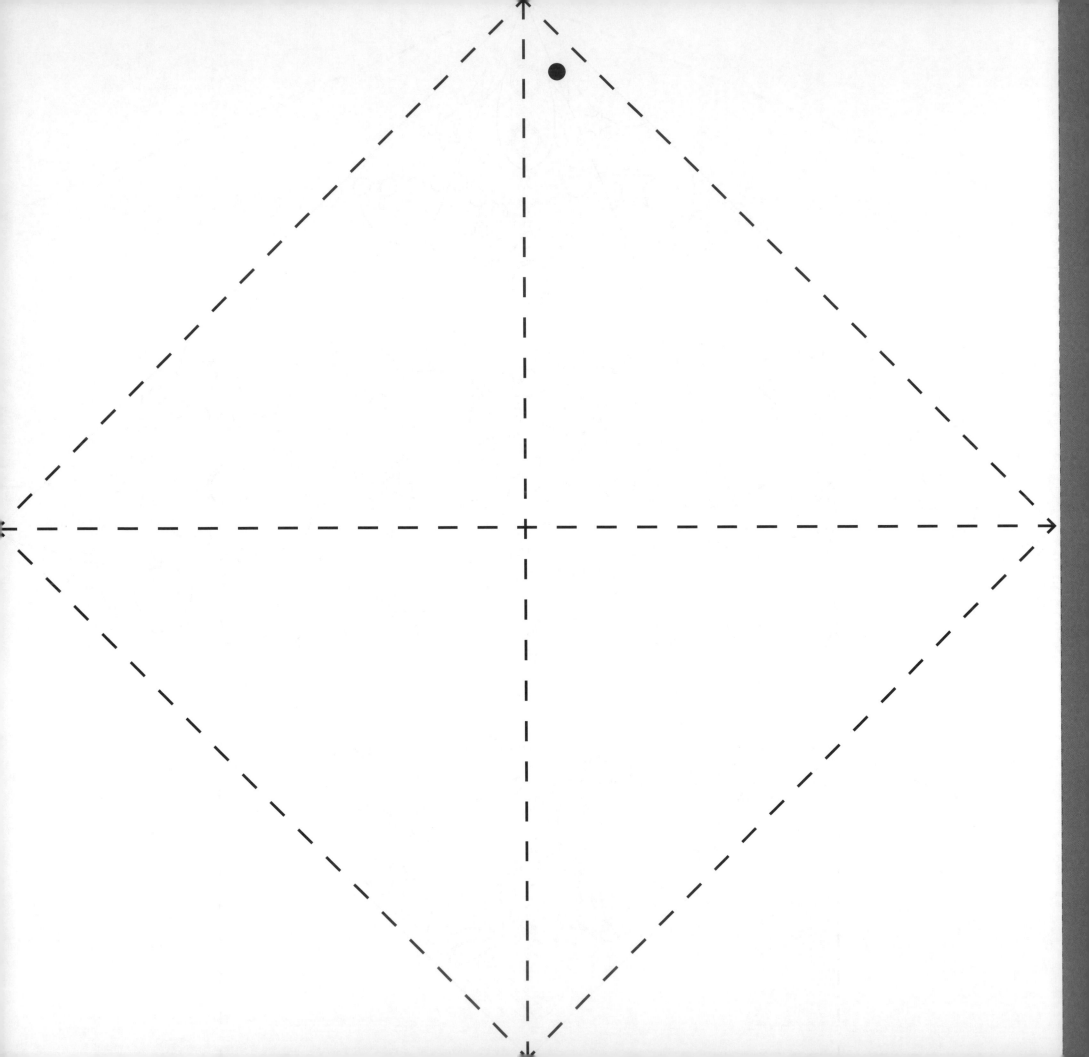

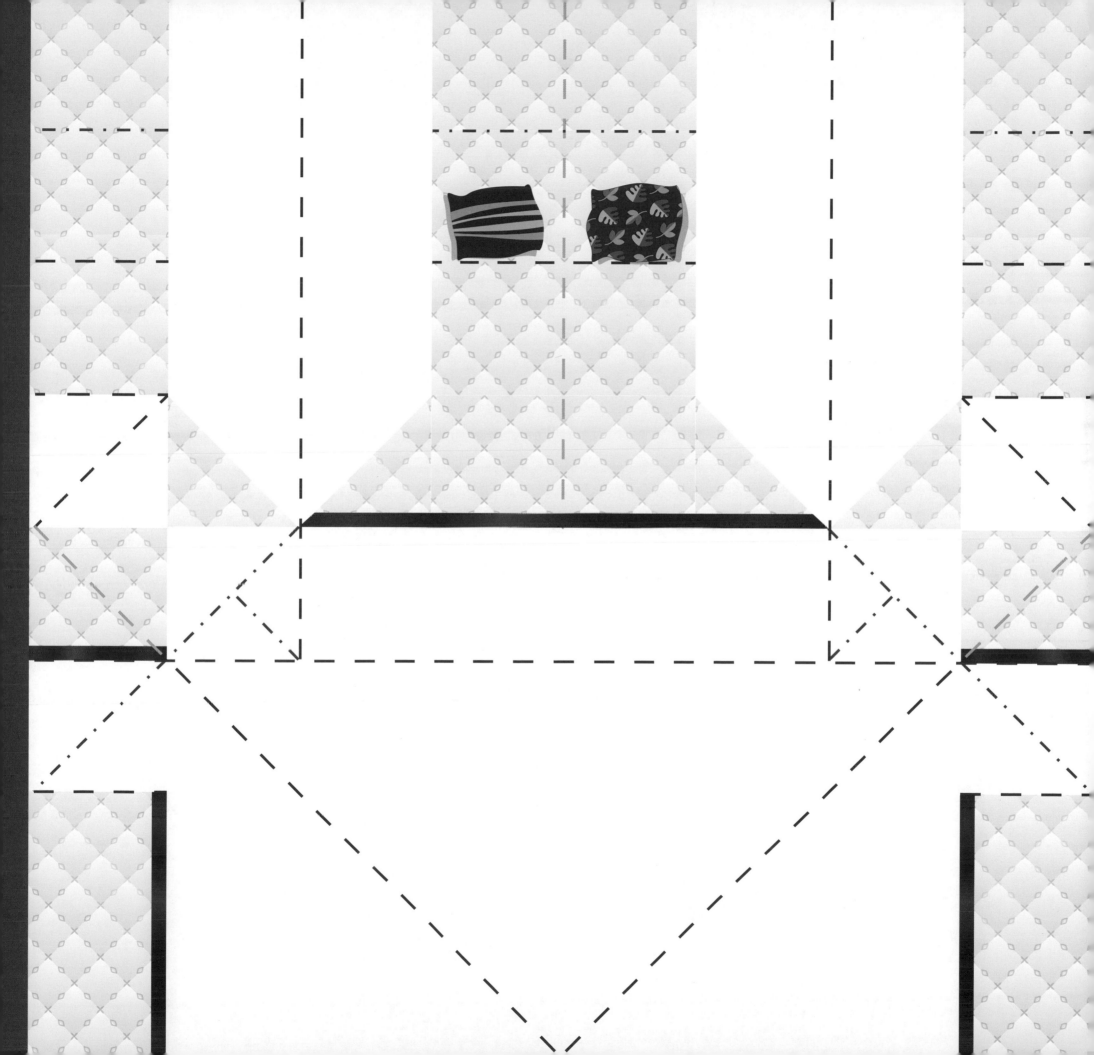